Emotional Holiness

EMOTIONAL HOLINESS

Discovering the Divine Plan for Your Human Emotions

By Abbot Austin G. Murphy, OSB

Our Sunday Visitor
Huntington, Indiana

Nihil Obstat
Msgr. Michael Heintz, Ph.D.
Censor Librorum

Imprimatur
✠ Kevin C. Rhoades
Bishop of Fort Wayne-South Bend
January 29, 2025

The *Nihil Obstat* and *Imprimatur* are official declarations that a book is free from doctrinal or moral error. It is not implied that those who have granted the *Nihil Obstat* and *Imprimatur* agree with the contents, opinions, or statements expressed.

Our Sunday Visitor Publishing Division
Our Sunday Visitor, Inc., 200 Noll Plaza, Huntington, IN 46750: www.osv.com; 1-800-348-2440

ISBN: 978-1-63966-215-9 (Inventory No. T2904)
1. RELIGION—Christian Living—Spiritual Growth.
2. RELIGION—Christian Living—Personal Growth.
3. RELIGION—Christianity—Catholic.

eISBN: 978-1-63966-216-6
LCCN: 2025934418

Cover and interior design: Chelsea Alt
Cover art: Unsplash

PRINTED IN THE UNITED STATES OF AMERICA

To my parents, Thomas and Marie Murphy

CONTENTS

Conversion as Reforming, Not Rejecting, the Emotions

···················· PRAYER ····················

Almighty God, without You we can do nothing for our
salvation. We ask You to bless us as we reflect on the task
of ongoing conversion and on the role of the emotions
within it. We ask this through the intercession of holy
Mary, the seat of wisdom, and through the intercession
of Saints Benedict and Scholastica. Through Christ our
Lord. Amen.

This book arose out of retreat talks given to monastic communities. Typically, the retreats were four or five days long,
and I would give one or two talks a day. Elements of this original
context appear now and again in the following chapters, but not
in a way that makes the book less useful for laypeople, priests,
and religious who do not belong to a monastic order.

How can talks originally given to monks and nuns speak to a
wider audience? Because monks and nuns experience very much

the same things that others do as they try to work out their salvation. This is especially so with the emotions. Like everybody else, monks and nuns wrestle with anger, fear, desire, and other emotions. This is why monastic authors have talked about the emotions since the beginning of Christian monasticism. This book draws on these and other authors in the Catholic tradition to discuss the emotions — in particular, to discuss how to form the emotions so they contribute to ongoing conversion.

In this book, I use the metaphor of a journey to speak about ongoing conversion. This metaphor is a simple and ancient one for speaking about conversion, and it is very helpful. One reason is that conversion is hard. Journeys can also be hard. They can be long and tiresome. That's the way it is sometimes with conversion: hard, long, and tiresome.

Conversion is also like a journey because it has a destination. It is bringing us to an endpoint — namely, to God. God is the goal of conversion. We can speak of attaining God in different ways, so as to bring out different facets of it. The monastic tradition likes to speak of reaching God in terms of reaching the kingdom of God. We see this in the prologue of the *Rule of Saint Benedict*. There, Saint Benedict speaks of our becoming dwellers in the tent of God's kingdom, and he says that, to get to the kingdom, we must run there by doing good deeds. Right before this, he says, "Having girded our loins with faith and the observance of good deeds, let us continue on the path of the gospel, following its lead, so that we may merit to see him 'who has called us into his kingdom.'" And Saint Benedict concludes the prologue with an exhortation to run the path of God's commands and to persevere until death, so that we may merit to be sharers in God's kingdom.

Saint Benedict addresses these words to his monks, but they apply to all Christians. For all of us, ongoing conversion is a journey to God or, we may say, to His kingdom. If we want to succeed on a journey, we need to keep our destination in mind. We need to know where we are going. Something similar is true with conversion. To succeed at conversion, we need to be mindful of God as our endpoint: easy to say but hard to do.

The Emotions and Conversion

For many years, I have been interested in how the Church Fathers and our Catholic tradition in general speak about the emotions. When the Tradition speaks of the emotions, it often uses the word *passions* (in Latin, *passiones*), and while the word *emotions* is not a perfect translation of the Latin *passiones*, I think that it is best for conveying to a modern audience what is generally being discussed here.

Many are surprised to hear that our Catholic tradition says anything at all about the emotions, but, in fact, it has a lot to say about them. And when people learn that the Catholic tradition has something to say about the emotions, many are surprised to learn that it has an appreciative view of them, seeing them not as negative but as valuable — indeed, indispensable — for conversion.

What do the emotions have to do with the journey that we are on, this journey of conversion that leads to the kingdom? A lot. According to Saint Augustine, the emotions — he preferred to call them *affections* — indicate whether we are moving forward or backward on the journey to God. He thus calls the affections "the feet" of the soul, for they carry us to or away from God, depending on whether they are rightly ordered. Saint Augustine tells us that the work of conversion must involve the reform of our emotions. In other words, conversion must entail getting our emotions in order and on track. The project of conversion does not mean or even imply that we eradicate the emotions or that we see them as negative factors needing to be suppressed; instead, they need to be reformed.

This reform can be described in different ways. We can speak of converting the emotions or purifying them or ordering them aright. Notice, too, that conversion in general requires dying and rising in Christ. This also applies to the emotions. Their reform will involve a sort of dying and rising. Furthermore, all this relies on the help of God's saving grace. And so, just as God's grace heals and elevates human nature, so it will work to heal our emotions and to elevate them.

The dominant view in Western Catholic theology has been that the emotions need to be reformed, rather than eradicated or suppressed. Again, this is surprising to many today, since the opposite is sometimes said. But if you read correctly major writers in Western Catholic theology, such as Saints Augustine, Bernard, and Thomas Aquinas, this is their view. For them, our moral growth depends on converting the emotions.

So, if we are to journey to God, we must work on our emotions. To be sure, we are not just a bundle of emotions. We have reason and free will. But still, we live and swim in our emotions, with their pushes and pulls. And these pushes and pulls affect our thinking and willing. The emotions, after all, run deep. Some emotions are superficial, to be sure, but others influence us profoundly. In short, the emotions are an important part of human life.

The importance of the emotions was known to ancient thinkers. That's why they said that the soul has a passionate part as well as a rational part, and the passionate part was sometimes subdivided further into the concupiscible and the irascible parts. We then have the three parts that make up Plato's tripartite view of the soul — a view that so many in the Christian Tradition, including the monastic tradition, followed. But let's leave aside the further division of the passionate part into the concupiscible and the irascible, and let's simply consider the main division between the rational and the passionate parts of the soul.

I think that there is a lot of wisdom in this division of the soul into a passionate part and a rational part, and I often think about how to explain this to people today. Here's one attempt.

We have in us a thinking part and a feeling part. Both are with us on the journey of life, and we surely experience both in life. Yet we do not always experience them working together. With my thinking part, I can identify something as being good. I see it as something I should do. For example, with my thinking part, I may see that I should serve the homeless. But when I approach a homeless man, I notice a pungent odor on him. The odor even makes me sick. And then the feeling part of my soul makes me want to run away from that man. My thinking part wants one thing; my feeling part pushes me in another direction.

Or consider the temptations to do things I know I should not do. My thinking part tells me not to do them, but my feeling part wants me to do them. For instance, my thinking part tells me not to eat more food; my feeling part, however, draws me to take more than I need. Or my thinking part says not to let fly from my lips an angry word, but my feeling part wants me to let it fly. Another example: With my thinking part, I know that I should deal calmly and charitably with an acquaintance of mine — perhaps a family member or a fellow monk — but still my feeling part is stirred to impatience and annoyance around the person. So, it is hard to treat that person charitably.

In sum, the thinking part in me and the feeling part in me do not always cooperate with each other. Doesn't Saint Paul speak in similar terms in Romans 7:15–25? However, what if the two parts worked together? Then we would be making progress. This is the aim of conversion, to get these parts of our souls, the thinking part and the feeling part, to work in the same direction. When they do, the emotions in the feeling part work with the mind, which is the thinking part. And when the two work together, then, as the chapters of this book will show, we move closer to God on the journey to His kingdom.

Emotions Are Rooted in Perceptions

Now, if this is a bit abstract, I promise that I will get more concrete in the coming chapters. There, I will speak of actual emotions, such as fear, hope, despair, and anger. And I will try to show how these emotions affect ongoing conversion. Since I will be speaking a lot about emotions, I want to give a brief definition of an emotion in this introduction. An emotion is a reaction that is felt — that is, it is a *felt reaction.* That means it is physiological reaction, not a cerebral or an abstract one. With the emotion, I am *moved.* And that movement is the emotion.

But the movement is a reaction. It is prompted by something. What prompts or gives rise to an emotion? A perception. An emotion is a reaction to a perception. It is a reaction to how we look at a thing in terms of its being good or bad and so forth. To give an example: Think about how children perceive Santa Claus in the shopping mall. Some children see Santa as a good person, and they rejoice to see him. Others see him as a bad person, a scary person, and they scream when forced to be near the man. The same Santa draws the emotion of joy and the emotion of fear, depending on how a child perceives him.

So, at the root of our emotions are perceptions, the ways we look at things. But sometimes the perceptions that we form are formed unthinkingly, even subconsciously. This makes them hard to see clearly. A person may therefore have an emotion, such as sorrow, and not understand why. At other times, we do see the perception that is giving rise to an emotion, and what is more, we may see that the perception is incorrect. It is not the right way of looking at something. But for all that, we still can't shake the perception.

Here's an example: I find myself very sad because my favorite sports team lost an important game. I can see that my sorrow is based on perceiving this loss as though it were a major tragedy in life. Of course, this perception is not correct, for while it may be bad in a certain sense that my sports team lost, it is not a major tragedy in life. Now, I can tell myself that the loss is not that big a deal and that I should not perceive it as such a tragedy, for it is only a sports game. But still, the perception remains, and I remain depressed. Even though I see that the perception is wrong, it persists, and in turn, so does the emotion it causes.

In sum, beneath every emotion is a perception, and sometimes the perception is hidden, and sometimes it is persistent, even though we try to get rid of it. When our perceptions are hidden in the shadows of our souls, we don't understand where our emotions are coming from. And even when our perceptions are not hidden, they can be stubborn and hard to change.

Yet correcting how we look at things — that is, how we perceive them — is key to getting our emotions correct. This is one reason why conversion is so hard. In our effort to reform our emotions, we must work at forming correct perceptions, and that is hard to do — harder than it might seem. In the following chapters, I'll have many things to say about this. But at the outset, I want to state clearly that working with the emotions can be very difficult and also confusing. So, while I will do my best to speak clearly about the emotions and their underlying perceptions in the chapters that follow, do not take this clear talk about the emotions to be a denial of their complexity, subtlety, or unwieldiness, for they certainly are complex, subtle, and unwieldy at times!

I should warn that this book will require work on your part. The emotions are a complex topic, and what I say about them can therefore be easily misunderstood. I aim to make the emotions understandable, and I use relatable examples. Still, in order that you may understand correctly the points I am making, I ask that you read this book charitably and try to grasp the truth behind my words, even if at first they seem wrong. In other words, I am asking you to work with me as I try to give insights into a complex topic. I think that if you do so, then, even if you end up disagreeing with me on some points, you will walk away with a better understanding of the emotions.

Misunderstanding can arise not only because of the complexity of the emotions but also because people use the same or similar terms in different ways. For example, I might speak of fear in a way that differs from how others speak of it. I encourage you to try to see how I am using the term in order to understand the points I am making. In a way, I am asking you to think with and within the ideas I am presenting, somewhat like trying on a pair of shoes and walking in them for a while to see how well they fit.

Two particular things are especially worth keeping in mind when I talk about the emotions. One is that every emotion has a good purpose. Of course, emotions can be misguided and urge us in the wrong directions. But still, given that we are viewing the emotions as something God has put into our human nature, we must also say that every emotion has a good purpose. Even fear, anger, sorrow, and despair have their good purposes, as will be discussed in chapters 1, 4, 5, and 6.

Another thing to keep in mind when I speak of a particular emotion is that the emotion can have a variety of forms. It is like speaking of the color green and realizing that there are dark greens, light greens, intensely vibrant greens, and so on. I name one color, but still there are different versions of that color. Likewise with the emotions: even one emotion can have different versions, so to speak. Thus, with the emotion of sorrow, there can be sadness, grief, or pain. With anger, there can be resentment, indignation, or rage. Fear can be terror, anxiety, or dread. Nor are these exhaustive lists of the different versions that each of these particular emotions can have.

Throughout this book, I will follow the list of eleven emotions found in the writings of St. Thomas Aquinas: love (or liking), desire, joy, hate (or disliking), aversion, sorrow, hope, daring, despair, anger, and fear. I see the variety of emotional reactions (or felt reactions) as ultimately falling within this list of eleven emotions. In the appendix, I describe these eleven emotions in a compact way with study exercises to help further comprehension. You may choose to read this summary of the eleven emotions first, before reading the chapters, but that is not necessary.

If you find that you have an understanding of the emotions different from the one in this book and your understanding has proven helpful for you, then do not abandon it. But also try to learn from how the emotions are understood here. Again, I am presenting the emotions as movements, or reactions, within us. As such, they move us to act in certain ways toward the situations we encounter in life. So, when the emotions are ordered correctly, they help us to act correctly in those situations. Sometimes people speak of the emotions as *feelings* and see them as telling us about ourselves. This is true, but the emotions also help us act correctly in the world around us. Recall that we are on a journey to the kingdom of God, and as Saint Benedict says, we make progress toward the kingdom by doing good. Rightly formed emotions help us to act in ways that are good and right, so that we may make progress toward God.

A Note about Availing Oneself of Psychological or Psychiatric Help

I do not say much in this book about availing oneself of psychological counseling or of psychiatric medicine. This should not, however, be taken as a denial that these professions can help. Let me say some things in this regard.

Sometimes people hesitate to avail themselves of psychological counseling or psychiatric medicine because they think, "But people in the past didn't have those things." This is true, but people in the past also did not have penicillin and other antibiotics. As a result, when certain infections arose, they had to suffer more harm from them than we have to suffer today. Is there anything wrong with receiving antibiotics today, even though people in the past did not have them? No. Likewise, we can be grateful that we have psychological and psychiatric helps to combat mental health problems today.

Another reason some people resist seeking psychological or psychiatric help is the sense that it would be a moral failure to do so. That is, they sense that their problems are simply moral ones, so they should be able to work them out on their own, without these professional helps. In response, here are a few things to consider. First, when we are ill, we first see whether we can treat the illness on our own, before going to the doctor. That is a reasonable approach. Still, if we cannot overcome the problem ourselves, we do eventually go to the doctor. Likewise, if after attempting to resolve problems in how we are thinking or feeling, we still find ourselves stuck in the same problems, then perhaps professional help should be sought. There may be something wrong that requires the help of a professional to fix.

Second, it is not a moral failure to seek the help of another person in order to do what is right. If that were the case, then seeking spiritual direction would be a moral failing. And, for that matter, so would reading this book or any other book on the spiritual life. Rather, part of making good moral decisions is knowing when to seek the help of others. Also, when it comes to psychological counseling, you do not need to have a major problem that first arises and needs to be addressed to benefit from such counseling. Sometimes it is simply helpful to talk to an experienced or trained person about what is going on inside oneself, in order to understand and work with these inner dynamics better. At the same time, for Catholics, it is worthwhile to find a counselor who understands and can work within our Catholic worldview.

Third, and related to what has already been said, seeking

psychological or psychiatric help is not an escape from the moral life. It is, in fact, a moral decision, for, as noted, part of good moral decision-making is knowing when to seek another's assistance. Further, when done rightly, this kind of help does not excuse us from the moral life and the task of conversion but better equips us to undertake them. We need a properly functioning thinking part and feeling part to undertake the work of moral conversion. If you are a runner and you break your ankle, you will seek medical help to heal it, so as to be ready to run again. Likewise, good psychological and psychiatric help will contribute to healing the thinking and feeling parts within us, so that we can better use them to run the race of God's commandments and to reach His kingdom.

The reason I do not say much in the following chapters about availing oneself of psychological or psychiatric help is that I am not a professional in those fields. I do occasionally draw on insights from modern counseling, and there is significant overlap between the traditional Catholic view of the emotions and cognitive behavioral therapy in psychological counseling. But still, I am not a trained mental health professional.

Finally, I should add that, while clinical psychology and psychiatry provide valuable insights into the emotions, there are also insights into the emotions from outside those fields. In particular, theology and philosophy offer rich insights into the emotions, and it is upon these insights that the current book is based. I have personally found such insights helpful, and I hope that readers of this book will also find them so. At the same time, I hope that those who experience emotional problems of the kind that psychological counseling or psychiatric medicine can uniquely help will avail themselves of those aids.

Whether or not one makes use of those aids, working with the emotions is not easy, and there are no quick-fix resolutions for some of the challenges we encounter in this area. After all, reforming the emotions is part of conversion, and conversion is not a quick-fix process. But the work of converting the emotions, even though difficult, is most worthwhile, for through this arduous work, we journey closer to God and His kingdom.

CHAPTER 1

What Is Fear Good For?

··········· PRAYER ···········

*Almighty God, make us whole. Sin has divided and frag-
mented us; it has caused disintegration within us. So, we
ask that through the sending of Your Spirit, You gather us
up and reintegrate us. Bring together the different parts
within us — our thoughts, wishes, and emotions — so
that we may do Your will and glorify You in all things.
Through Christ our Lord. Amen.*

I once had a professor who said that we all fear things, but the
question is what we fear. Do we fear what we should fear, or are
we fearing things we should not be fearing?

The professor's thinking is in line with the view of conversion described in the introduction to this book. The project of
conversion entails not eradicating or suppressing the emotions
but getting them rightly ordered. So, in the case of the emotion
of fear, we are not seeking to get rid of fear in this life, but we
want it to work in the right direction for us.

A quick note to avoid misunderstanding: When I say that

we are not to eradicate or suppress the emotions, I do not mean that we are to follow whatever they tell us to do. No, that would be disaster! Rather, we want to *convert* the emotions. And part of conversion is dying so as to rise to new life. So, our emotions are to die — but not to be eradicated or suppressed forever. They must die so that they may rise again in Christ.

So it is with the emotion of fear. It has its good purpose, and we want to convert our fear to its good purpose. This is not to say that every particular fear is to be saved and transformed. No, there are bad instances of fear (such as excessive anxiety), and we should overcome them as much as possible, sometimes taking advantage of psychological or psychiatric resources to do so. Rather, we are talking about working with our natural capacity to fear in a way that harnesses that capacity, so that, instead of trying to suppress all fears in our lives, we cultivate good and healthy fears that help us in our journey to God.

In our culture, fear is often presented in a bad light. And what is more, there are passages in Scripture that tell us not to fear. So, you would be excused if you thought that fear is always bad.

Before looking at Scripture, we can note some negative views of fear in our culture. There is the celebrated line from Franklin Delano Roosevelt: "The only thing we have to fear is fear itself." And the following statement is often attributed to Gandhi: "The enemy is fear. We think it is hate; but it is really fear." Here fear is presented not only as bad, but as the enemy!

I think that this view of fear — as the enemy — is prevalent in our society. Some would trace all bad behaviors and bad attitudes back to fear. I know a very smart, insightful man who takes this approach. Whenever he sees bad behavior, he asks what the people exhibiting the behavior are afraid of. For him, fear is always at the root of the bad behavior. The implication is that if we could just eradicate the fear, we could eliminate the bad behavior.

Now, this may *often* be the case, but I don't think it is *always* the way to resolve a problem. After all, shouldn't we be afraid of some things? And if we should, then the real problem is not fear itself but fearing the wrong things. We want to make sure we don't fear in a bad way, but only in the right way.

As noted, there are biblical teachings against fear. But we should also notice that there are biblical teachings that tell us that we *should* fear. As for teachings against fear, there is the teaching of the First Letter of John 4:18, which Saint Benedict invokes at the end of the steps of humility in his *Rule*. The teaching is that when we arrive at perfect love, this love casts out fear. And of course, the Lord himself often says, "Do not be afraid."

I think these teachings show that there is a kind of fear we are to avoid or to grow out of. To be sure, in the next life, when the kingdom of heaven has been fully established, there will be nothing to fear. But in this life, while we are on the journey, there is a place for a healthy kind of fear.

As for good fear, the psalmist says, "The fear of the LORD is the beginning of wisdom" (Ps 111:10; see also Prv 9:10; 15:33). And Christ hjimself says, "And do not fear those who kill the body but cannot kill the soul; rather fear him who can destroy both soul and body in hell" (Mt 10:28).

A Healthy Fear

So, what is a good and healthy fear? I would identify two conditions. The first has to do with the perception that triggers the fear. Remember, an emotion stems from a perception. What perception, then, does fear stem from?

Fear arises when we perceive that something bad is threatening to happen. It is not just that something bad *can* happen but that it is *threatening* to happen. For example, while I am driving a car, there is a possibility that I will get into an accident. That is a bad thing that can happen. But this does not typically lead to fear in normal driving conditions. Yet when the roads are very icy, then the bad thing — a car accident — is actually a threat, not just a remote chance. Fear then arises.

So, fear arises when we perceive that something bad is threatening to happen, not just that it *can* happen. We may say this more concisely as follows: Fear arises when we perceive a danger. That's the perception underlying fear, the perception of a danger.

Accordingly, for fear to be good and appropriate, there must actually be a danger at hand. It needs to be reality based. Fear is not appropriate when there is no real danger. So, to return to the example of children and Santa Claus mentioned in the introduction, being afraid of Santa Claus in a mall is not a correct fear because Santa is not a real danger. The first condition, then, for a fear to be good and healthy is that there is, in fact, a real danger at hand.

That being the case, the good thing about fear is that it makes us alert to the danger. Our senses and thinking are heightened so that we pay attention to how to avoid the danger. This is good. When there is a real danger, we want to be alert.

But we know that sometimes fear is excessive. For example, fear can paralyze a person. Then the person is not alert but inert. And that, of course, is not good. Sometimes this happens with public speaking. I'm a shy person myself, and back in my school days, I hated when I had to get up in front of the class to give a presentation. Not only did I hate it; I feared that I would look stupid or say something wrong. I can appreciate how such a fear can paralyze a person, even to the point of being unable to speak.

That's one way that fear can be excessive, by paralyzing us. Another way is by causing us to overreact. A soldier who crosses enemy lines should have fear, a healthy fear that makes him alert to the danger at hand. But if the fear makes him overreact, so that he panics and starts firing his gun at random, that is not good.

So, the second condition for a healthy fear is that it is not excessive, so that it does not paralyze us or make us overreact. True, we might imagine a fear that is too weak rather than excessive. For example, the person driving on icy roads may be afraid of a car accident, but the person should have greater fear so as to be more alert. However, fear usually errs in the other direction, by being excessive rather than deficient. So, the second condition for a healthy fear is that it not be excessive so as to cause paralysis or panic. A healthy fear, instead, makes a person alert, so as to avoid the danger.

In sum, the two conditions for good, healthy fear are: first, there is a real danger at hand, not an imagined one; and second, the fear makes one alert and is not excessive in its reaction.

Two Examples of Bad Fear Plus a Healthy Fear Not to Be Followed

Ultimately, I want us to reflect on how a healthy fear helps with conversion and the journey to God. But first, I want us to exercise our minds by thinking through some examples of fear. Two examples I provide here are of fearing in wrong ways. The third example is for the sake of making a worthwhile distinction.

The first example: I don't know whether you believe in ghosts, but here's a ghost story that I experienced. The campus of the high school that my abbey founded used to be an orphanage. In fact, on the campus is a cemetery for some orphans who died in residence.

Moreover, when I worked at the high school as campus minister, I shared an office with the outreach director. And the story was that this office used to be where they kept the bodies of deceased orphans before their burial! What is more, there were stories of ghost appearances in the building. At one point, a man who used to work in maintenance at the high school told me about hearing voices and seeing silhouettes of little children during the night, when no students could have been in the building.

I shrugged off these stories, but not long after hearing this last one, I was working late one night at the high school. I was at my desk, which was in the back of the office, away from the doorway. It was about midnight.

Outside my door I heard in the hallway what sounded like footsteps — thump, thump, thump, thump. I started to get scared and tried to put out of my head the thought that some ghost was walking outside my office. But the thought came back, and I was feeling fear. This went on for a while: The thought of a ghost was on my mind, and I was experiencing fear, and I tried to expel that thought from my mind, thinking how ridiculous it was.

Eventually, I couldn't put up with it anymore. I decided to walk to my door, muster up my nerve, and then look into the hallway. And so I did. I saw nothing. Yet the noise was still there. So I ventured farther down the hall. Still nothing but the noise of footsteps.

Having searched the hall and found nothing, I turned around and went back toward my office. And then I discovered the source of the noise. The old wooden door to the room opposite my office didn't fit snuggly in the doorframe. Since the window in the room was open, it was pushing the old door out, so it tapped against the doorframe and made sounds just like footsteps in the hallway.

So, in this case, it turned out that I had fear that was not founded. There was no real danger — no ghosts of dead orphans in the building. But this story does show how stubborn our perceptions can be. The perception that there might be a ghost would not go away, even though I kept telling myself that that was ridiculous. The perception stayed there, and in turn, it led me to have fear.

Now, a second example of fearing in a wrong way: In the Gospel, when Herold learns from the Magi that a king has been born, he is afraid of losing power to this king. Eventually, this fear leads him to commit murder. Is his fear a healthy one? Of course not. For one, it is excessive, leading him to do what is unjust — murder. But also, there is no real danger for him to fear. Christ is not after his earthly throne. A lot could be said about this fear, but I think you get the point.

Lastly, what about the fear of being rejected or persecuted if you do what is right? I once heard the story of a teenage boy who was shot and killed in a mall outside Washington, DC. Why? Because he refused to join a gang. So, the gang shot him to make a point.

When this brave young man didn't join the gang, was he afraid that he might be targeted as a result? I imagine that he had such a fear. That would be natural. But what should we make of such a fear? Would it have been a good, healthy fear or a bad, unhealthy one?

So far, I have presented a healthy fear as one that makes us alert so as to avoid a danger. Thus, there is a healthy fear of a car accident when the roads are icy, and that fear helps a person to drive more carefully, so as to avoid an accident. And a soldier has a healthy fear while in battle, and that fear helps him to be alert, so as to avoid being injured by the enemy.

But in the case of this young man, his fear did not cause him to avoid the danger. It did not, for example, lead him to join the gang so as to avoid being targeted by them. What, then, was the purpose of this fear? What good did it do him if it did not help him avoid the danger? And if the fear did not do him good, can we call it a good fear?

We don't want to call it a bad fear, for it is perfectly understandable and natural. And it does satisfy the two conditions for being a healthy fear. It was a response to a real danger, not an imagined one. And the fear was not excessive by making the young man overreact or become paralyzed. Perhaps, then, it was a healthy fear. Again, it was surely natural and understandable.

What we see in this case is that sometimes a fear is natural and understandable, but it is not to be acted upon. The fear makes us alert to a real danger, but we are not to avoid the danger. We are to face it bravely — just as this young man did.

Notice the distinction here between having the emotion of fear and acting on it. When we have a fear that is not healthy, we surely should not act upon it. But sometimes even when our fear is healthy, we are not to act upon it, meaning we are not to let it lead us away from the danger.

I wonder if this helps us to understand Jesus' words: "Do not be afraid." It's not so much that we should not experience the emotion of fear but that we shouldn't act out of the fear in question. "Do not be afraid" then means, "Do not give in to the emotion of fear when it would lead you astray." You may have the emotion of fear when you see that you will suffer for doing the right thing, but do not let that fear cause you to avoid doing the right thing.

Fear may pulse through your body in such a situation. Maybe it did for some of the martyrs when they were arrested and saw what was coming. We hear that some martyrs displayed no such fear but were joyful at the hour of their deaths. It was, in fact, their executioners who trembled! But perhaps some of the martyrs in the history of the Church felt fear. Even so, they did not let fear have the last say over their actions. They still bravely endured their suffering. They followed Christ's teaching not to be afraid in the sense that they did not let fear take control of them, to cause them to depart from the difficult but correct path.

We can return here to Jesus' teaching mentioned earlier: "And do not fear those who kill the body but cannot kill the soul; rather fear him who can destroy both soul and body in hell" (Mt 10:28). I want to suggest that we might find in this teaching a way in which a healthy fear, even when it is not to be followed, can have a good purpose.

Recall that fear makes us alert to the danger at hand. It thus makes us think carefully about the danger. That is, a healthy fear heightens not only our senses but our thinking. In turn, we give careful attention to the matter at hand. And when we do give careful attention to the matter, we may see the logic in Jesus' teaching. What is the greater danger that we should fear? Is it the persons who can harm our bodies, or is it the danger of having soul and body destroyed by disobeying God?

A healthy fear can cause us to think carefully about this and to see that the danger from disobeying God is greater. We are to fear disobeying God more than fearing the persecution of men. This is, of course, a hard teaching, but it is true. A healthy fear of persecution may lead us to see the truth of this teaching by making us think carefully about the matter. In that way, the fear serves a purpose. It leads us to have a deeper fear, a fear of a greater danger — that of displeasing God — and this deeper fear helps us to do the right thing.

In the end, what we want to do is cultivate our emotions, including the emotion of fear, so that we do not have to act against them. Instead, we want them to push and pull us in the right directions. We want to train our emotions so that they give us a facility in doing right.

So it is with our fears. We don't want them to make it more difficult for us to do the right thing — although at times some fears will understandably do that. What we want is to cultivate the kind of fear that makes it easier to do the right thing.

Fear While on the Journey

So, is there a kind of fear that can help us in our journey to the kingdom of God? Yes, there is. To see this, consider again the two conditions for a healthy fear. The first is that there is a real danger at hand. So, let us ask: Is there a real danger in this life, as we journey to God? Yes, the real danger is that we will sin and stray from the path leading to the kingdom.

This is a real danger because we are weak and we easily fall into sin. There are vices that we can easily fall into, vices such as impatience, anger, possessiveness, lust, spiritual laziness, and self-admiration. These are real dangers.

And fear is good if it makes us alert to these dangers so as to avoid them. Recall what Christ says in the Gospel passage that we read on the First Sunday of Advent: "Take heed, watch and pray" (Mk 13:33). There is a danger we might fall asleep and not be ready when the Lord comes — whether His coming is at the time of our death or at the end of time. We must stay alert, therefore, because we have within us the ability to fall away from God.

Again and again, the Lord warns us against this — for instance, in the parable of the wise and foolish virgins, the parable of the sheep and the goats, the parable of the talents, and many others. He warns us to be ready, for there is a danger that we will not be ready.

So, I would argue that there is a healthy fear for us on the journey. In his *Rule*, Saint Benedict highlights this fear for the abbot of the monastery, saying that he should care not only about his own tendency to stray but also about that tendency among the sheep entrusted to him. But for this fear to be healthy, it must not be excessive. The fear of straying from God should neither paralyze us nor make us overreact in the spiritual life. We thus satisfy the second condition of a healthy fear: that the fear makes us alert without making us panic or paralyzing us.

Advent and the Reform of Fear

I see the season of Advent as especially related to the reform of our fear. I know that many people associate Advent with hope and expectation. And it surely is about that. But I think it also helps us to reform the emotion of fear.

As I just mentioned, the Gospel for the First Sunday of Advent tells us to be watchful and alert. And it is fear, a healthy fear, that brings about this alertness in the spiritual life. The two themes of Advent are the First and Second Comings of Christ. When we begin Advent, the Second Coming of the Lord at the end of time is in the forefront. We recall how Jesus will come as Judge to establish definitively the kingdom of God. The other coming, the First Coming of Jesus as a child to save us, comes especially to the fore as we get closer to Christmas.

We seem to give more attention to the First Coming during Advent, even to the point of neglecting the Second Coming. A few years ago, I was at a parish speaking about Advent, and a woman in the audience told me that she never knew that the Second Coming of Christ was a theme in Advent. I don't think that she is alone. And yet the Church, in her instructions about the liturgical year, says that the two comings of Christ — the First and the Second — are the themes of Advent.

One reason we might not think about the Second Coming is that it is a bit scary. It frightens us — that is, it causes fear. While it may not be pleasant, it is good for the Second Coming to stir fear within us. That's because we then have to ask ourselves, "Why am I afraid?" In one of his sermons on the Psalms, Saint Augustine asks this question: Why are we afraid to think about the return of Christ? Don't we love Him? And if we love Him, shouldn't we look forward to His return?

Of course, we are afraid because we do not always act as servants who are ready for the Master's return. Sometimes we are negligent or halfhearted in our Christian service to God and neighbor. Therefore, we experience fear when we think of the Lord returning to judge us.

And that is good, at least as a starting point. It alerts us to the need to be better servants. It reawakens us to the task of discipleship, to that work of conversion. As Saint Benedict says, "Let us get up then, at long last, for the Scriptures rouse us when they say: 'It is high time for us to arise from sleep' (Rom 13:11)."

How to Understand What It Means to Fear God

I would like to say something about how the Bible speaks of fearing God. I have just said that we fear when we perceive a danger at hand. But, of course, when the Bible speaks of fearing God, it is not because God is the danger to be avoided.

I like to think of this in relation to the Church's teaching on perfect and imperfect contrition. Imperfect contrition is, as we know, sorrow for our sins because of the fear of the punishments they deserve. Perfect contrition is sorrow for our sins because they offend the God we love. Perfect contrition is, of course, better. But the wonderfully merciful thing is that God accepts even imperfect contrition, and so imperfect contrition suffices for receiving absolution when we go to confession. Still, we should move toward perfect contrition.

We can think likewise about the danger of sinning that leads to fear. On the one hand, we might fear sin because we see the danger as that of being punished for sinning. But even better, we should see the danger of sin as that of offending God, and that pains us because we love God.

Yet whether it is the danger of punishment or the danger of offending God, when we speak of fearing God, the danger is not God himself, "who is all good and deserving of all my love" (as one form of the act of contrition has it). He's not the danger; the root of the danger is my own sinful weakness.

This danger is real, so there is a healthy fear that goes with it. And if this fear is healthy, it will not paralyze us or make us overreact. Instead, it will make us alert, so as to avoid the danger posed by our tendency to sin.

If we are alert to this danger, then the question becomes: How can we avoid it? The answer is by turning to the Lord for mercy. Without the Lord, what hope would we have? Without the graces offered through Jesus, how could we be saved? But we know that in the Lord there is mercy and fullness of redemption (see Ps 130:7). And through faith in the humanity of Jesus Christ, we receive that saving mercy.

Notice a few things about God's mercy. Most obviously, God in His mercy forgives us our failings. But also, His mercy sets us on the path to the kingdom. Some people see God's mercy as saying to us: "I forgive you; now you can go do whatever you want." But, of course, that is not the case. God's mercy gives us a direction, and this is something to be thankful for! It's not pleasant being without a direction in life. So, when God forgives us in His mercy, He also, in His mercy, gives us a direction, a way in which to walk. He sets us anew on the journey that leads to Him.

Recall the blind man who is healed in the Gospel and immediately follows Christ. The Gospel text says, "Immediately he received his sight and followed [Jesus] on the way" (Mk 10:52). So too, God's mercy not only forgives us but also sets us on the journey to Him.

Finally, God's mercy gives us the graces we need to walk the journey successfully. God, in His mercy, gives us the helps we need to keep at the journey and to finish it. So, the divine mercy does these three things: It forgives us, it sets us anew on the path leading to God, and it sustains us on that path.

A healthy fear in the spiritual life makes us turn to God's mercy. We see the real danger posed by our sinful tendencies and, as a result, we turn to the Lord for help. We call upon the name of the Lord, who is quick to save us. This turning to the Lord is at the heart of conversion. In fact, the very word *conversion* means a "turning to." Fear awakens us, so we once again turn to God for mercy.

I find it interesting that fear is often mentioned as the first step in conversion. Recall the biblical teaching that fear of the Lord is the beginning of wisdom (see Ps 111:10; Prv 9:10; 15:33).

Also, saints have spoken of fear as the beginning of making progress toward God.

I mentioned earlier how the Advent theme of the Second Coming of Christ can arouse this healthy fear in us. When this fear causes us to turn to God for mercy, the other Advent theme — Christ's First Coming — is all the more appreciated. In the First Coming, we see the great mercy of God. When God comes to us as a child and shows that He is with us, the kindness of God appears to us, as the Letter of Saint Paul to Titus says (3:4). We see the mercy of God before our eyes! When we know our weakness and how much we need God's help, this appearance of God among us is a most welcome sight.

....

Glory be to the Father and to the Son and to the Holy Spirit;
as it was in the beginning, is now, and ever shall be, world
without end. Amen.

CHAPTER 2

Learning to Like God

When I was in seminary, the professor who taught preaching told us not to use the word *love* in our homilies. Besides being overused, the word can mean too many things. Thus, if a preacher uses it, the meaning will not be clear, and people may think he means something he does not mean.

I take my professor's rule to be like the rule "Never say never." It is a bit tongue-in-cheek and is not to be taken literally, but still, it makes a point. The point is that when we use the word *love*, we should be mindful of its wide range of meanings. One can use the word to say many things, such as "I love God," "I love my neighbor," "I love my spouse," "I love ice cream," "I love your shoes," "I love this weather," "I love my dog," "I love that song,"

"I love it when things go my way," and "I love it when my enemy fails." You get the point! Ideally, the English language would have a rich variety of words to cover these different kinds of love, but it does not.

And yet we must talk about love. The two greatest commandments, says Jesus, are to love the Lord your God with all your heart, all your soul, and all your mind and to love your neighbor as yourself (see Mt 22:37–40; Mk 12:29–31; Lk 10:26–28). Our salvation depends on loving. We must love in the way that Jesus showed us. Another reason we must talk about love is that it is the most fundamental emotion. All other emotions are based on it. In his *City of God*, Saint Augustine goes so far as to say that every emotion is an expression of a love.

Now, you might be wondering, "If love is the most fundamental emotion, why didn't we cover it in the first chapter?" For one, I began with fear instead because there is a tradition of seeing fear as the beginning of a conversion process, as mentioned in the previous chapter. But also, the emotion of love is a more subtle emotion to discuss than other emotions. Therefore, by cutting our teeth first with the emotion of fear, we are better prepared to discuss now the emotion of love. Given that it is the basis of all the emotions, our efforts to reform our emotions must eventually address it. Indeed, the project of reforming what we love must be a fundamental part of reforming the emotions.

Love as an Emotion Versus as an Act of the Will

But in saying that love is the basis of all the emotions, we run into the problem I just mentioned: What kind of love do I mean? To clarify, I am speaking of love as an emotion, which is distinct from love as an act of the will. The two influence each other and often work together when we love something or someone. But they do not always work together, and so they can be distinguished. When we speak of love as an act of the will, we can define it as willing the good of the other, particularly if we are talking about loving our neighbor. But the emotion of love is different.

As an emotion, love is what we mean when we say that we *like* something, whether it be a kind of food, a type of music, or a particular person. To like something is to have the emotion of love toward it. Speaking of the emotion of love as liking is not a perfect way to speak about the emotion. For one thing, the word *like* (or *liking*) often makes people think of a superficial love for something, whereas the emotion of love can run very deep. Still, even though not perfect, this is a helpful way of speaking about the emotion of love, and I will use it here.

Put this way, we can more easily see the difference between love as an emotion and love as an act of the will. For instance, notice that we must love people even when we do not like them. Even happily married couples will not like each other on some days, but they still need to love each other on those days. In a monastery, some monks do not like each other, but they should love each other. In fact, sometimes we do not even like ourselves, but still we must love ourselves.

To be sure, to love with the will is more important than to like with an emotion. In other words, our primary responsibility is to love correctly with the will. We have less control over what we like, so we are less responsible for it. What we like is still important, however, for the reason mentioned above — namely, that the emotion of liking is the basis of all the other emotions. So, if we want to reform our emotions, it is especially important to reform the emotion of liking.

Before we go any further, though, perhaps we should test the claim that the emotion of love or liking is the basis of all the other emotions. For instance, some might say that the emotion of desire is the most basic emotion there is, not the emotion of love. Well, it depends on what we mean by *desire*. Sometimes we speak of love and desire interchangeably, so that the words *love* and *desire* refer to the same thing. But it is possible to make a distinction between the two, and when we do, the primacy of love or liking emerges.

Here is how the distinction works. When you love or like something but do not have it, then you desire it. So, desire applies when you do not have the thing that you like. But what happens when you do have the thing that you like? Then you have the emotion of joy. So, joy occurs when you possess what you like; desire occurs when you do not possess it. As an example, suppose I have a liking for hamburgers. If I do not have a hamburger to eat, then I desire one, but when I do eat one, I enjoy it. Or suppose I like spending time with a friend. If that friend moves away, I then experience the desire to be with the friend again. And if I am reunited with the friend, then I have joy. Notice that whether you have joy or desire, you continually have the emotion of liking. In this way, liking is even more fundamental than desiring.

Here is another objection to the claim that liking is the most fundamental emotion. It is not that there is a *more* fundamental emotion but that there is *another* fundamental emotion as well. It is the emotion of disliking, which is also called the emotion of hate. So, the objection says that *not every* emotion is based on liking something, for *some* emotions are instead based on disliking something. For example, you experience the emotion of fear when what you dislike threatens to happen. It has nothing to do with what you like, only with what you dislike, and therefore, it arises not from the emotion of liking but from the emotion of disliking.

There is some truth to this objection. Some emotions are reactions to things you dislike. And for that reason, you can speak of certain emotions as being based on disliking. In fact, I will sometimes speak that way. But there is still a sense in which the emotion of love or liking is more fundamental than that of hate or disliking.

To see this, we must look at the larger project we are involved in. We are seeking the things that will bring us joy. We cannot help it. That is simply how we have been made by God. We have been made for joy. Yes, we are made for *true* joy, not for bad versions of joy that ultimately do not satisfy, but we can leave that issue aside for now. For now, we note that we are seeking the things that will bring us joy, and as just mentioned, we experience joy when we attain the things that we like. Thus, we are trying to attain the things we like so that we will have joy in them.

But we cannot say the same for the things we dislike. We are trying not to attain them but to avoid them. And what is more, we are avoiding the things we dislike for the sake of attaining the things that we alternatively do like. So, I avoid eating something I dislike, such as chopped liver, for the sake of eating what I do like, a hamburger. And I avoid spending free time with people I dislike in order to spend it with people I do like. The reverse is not true. I do not attain what I like (such as a hamburger) for the sake of avoiding the thing I dislike (the chopped liver). In other words, the sought-after end is to rest joyfully in the attainment of what we like. It is not to avoid what we dislike, for once we do that, we do not rest, but we move on to attain what we like. Attainment is an end in itself, whereas avoidance is not.

This is why liking is more fundamental than disliking. The larger project we find ourselves in is to identify and attain what we like, and that, rather than finding what we dislike, sets the agenda. So, the most fundamental emotion we must reform is the emotion of liking. To the extent we do, we set the foundation on which the other emotions can be built up correctly. But to the extent we fail to do this, the other emotions are off-kilter from the start.

Are We Responsible for What We Like?

But is it even possible to reform the emotion of liking? Can we reform what we like or do not like? Isn't it rather the case that we simply like something or do not like it? It is similar to one's tastes: Something tastes good to us, or it doesn't. As the old Latin saying has it, *De gustibus non est disputandum* (There is no arguing about tastes).

There is, of course, some truth to this. But it is also true that some of our likes can be reformed — and should be. After all, we don't want to let ourselves off the hook too easily here. Suppose, for example, that I like to see people fail. Having a liking for this says something about me, something negative. I shouldn't just accept that, but I should work at it, so that I no longer like such a thing.

To understand this better, let's look at the perception that underlies the emotion of love or liking. It is the perception that something agrees with me. I find the thing agreeable, and thus, I like it. Right away, we can observe the complexity that this introduces. Things can be agreeable in different ways, and the same thing might even be agreeable in one respect and disagreeable in another. For example, suppose I love ice cream but I am lactose intolerant. So, I find ice cream agreeable to my taste, but I find it disagreeable to my digestion. I like ice cream in one respect and dislike it in another. In turn, I feel conflicted. My liking for the taste of ice cream pulls me toward eating it, but as I remember the indigestion this has caused me in the past, I have a dislike for eating ice cream that pushes me away from eating it.

It is possible that, after suffering digestive problems many times, I lose my liking for ice cream. In turn, I would only have a strong disliking for it and no longer be drawn to it. But it could also happen that I retain a liking for ice cream, even while I also dislike ice cream. In this case, I am always going to experience a tension within me between liking ice cream and disliking it. A similar tension exists, for example, in those who love to smoke cigarettes but hate the adverse health effects.

So, let's return to the question: Can we reform what we like and dislike? There are going to be some likes that do not go away, even though we try. And these might not be likes that are superficial, such as liking ice cream, but likes that are deep-seated. To give an example, a man I know shared with me that he is a narcissist. He said that he has learned how to manage this through therapy. So, this man has a deep-seated liking for positive attention, so much so that it has created major problems in his life. Positive attention is something that he is always going to like, and he has to manage it.

I admire this man because he has learned to manage it. I knew him for a while before he shared with me his diagnosis as a narcissist, and I would never have guessed this about him. That's how effectively he has learned to manage his deep liking and even craving for positive attention.

In this example, we see a deep-seated, disordered liking that will not go away. This man will always like positive attention in a disordered way. But notice that the man learned to dislike this disordered liking, and this provided motivation for him not to act on it. Indeed, we can say that this disliking that he developed was based on a more fundamental liking. He came to like his life when it was not governed by narcissism. He cultivated an emotional love, or liking, for his non-narcissistic way of life. Thus, with these emotions of liking and disliking, he has the emotional energy to manage his narcissism.

The point is that we can form and develop what we like and what we dislike, even when we are unable to change the fact that we like something in a disordered way. That is, even when we have a deep-seated liking for the wrong thing and this disordered liking will not go away, we can cultivate likes and dislikes that help us to resist the urgings of the disordered liking. To live with such a tension is, of course, a cross. It is a "thorn in the flesh," to use Saint Paul's expression in 2 Corinthians 12:7. Still, with the help of God's grace, we should develop a disliking for the disordered liking. It's not that we hate ourselves, but we hate or dislike the disordered liking, since it works against our true selves. Thus, what we do like is our true selves. We cultivate an emotional liking for what our lives are like when, not following the disordered liking, we live according to our true selves.

Loving and Liking God

Reforming what we like and what we dislike is not only for the sake of resisting disordered likings that would lead us astray from the path to God. It is also, and ultimately, for the sake of liking God himself. If we cultivate the emotion of love or liking for God, this will help us on the journey to God. As I have said, the emotion of liking sets the direction for the rest of the emotions. So, by developing a liking for God, we get the other emotions to support us in trying to attain God as well as in trying to avoid what keeps us from Him.

The pursuit of God must first and foremost be led by loving God as an act of the will. The emotion of liking God cannot lead the way but must work alongside and under the guidance of this love. One reason the will's act of loving God must lead the way is that there will be times when we do not have an emotional liking for God. During these times, we still must love God with the will — as we must love someone even when we do not like that person. The emotion of liking comes and goes, but the will's love must remain constant.

And yes, it is possible not to like God. That is, we can lack an emotional liking for God. For example, have you ever lacked the motivation to pray? I have. In those times, the emotional part of my soul resists spending time in prayer. I do not feel like praying. Sometimes my emotional or feeling part even finds prayer tedious, so that not only do I lack an attraction to it, but I am repelled by it. Now, what is prayer but an opportunity to be in the presence of God? So, if I liked being with God, I would be attracted to prayer with the emotional part of my soul. And yet sometimes I am not, and this suggests that, during these times, I am lacking in an emotional love for God.

Of course, the reality can be more complex. One can find prayer both attractive and repulsive at the same time. It is like ice cream for a lactose-intolerant person: The same thing is found to be agreeable in one respect while disagreeable in another. So, one likes prayer — that is, one finds it agreeable because one likes God, and prayer is a chance to be with Him. But at the same time, one finds prayer disagreeable. Finding prayer disagreeable need not be due to any sinful inclination. It might simply be that one is restless or stir-crazy after a long day of sitting at a desk for work and thus dislikes the idea of sitting still any longer in order to pray. Whatever the reason, one finds prayer disagreeable in some respect, and the consequent disliking for prayer is in conflict with one's liking for prayer. So, there is a tension. One is divided, and that division within oneself weakens one's motivation to pray.

We need not get discouraged by our lack of motivation for prayer or by the fact that sometimes our emotional love for God is lacking. Our emotions are fickle, and we cannot always ensure that they will be the way we wish. That is why we must make sure to love God with our will, even when the emotional love is lacking. In fact, there may be times when we not only lack an emotional liking for God, but we dislike Him in some respect. This happens, for example, when a person is angry with God about something. Whatever the case, the fact is that when the emotional love or liking for God is lacking, it becomes harder to do the right thing, such as spend time in prayer. At these times, we still need to love God with our will and to use the power of our wills — that is, our willpower — to push through in doing what is right.

When this is the case, it can seem as if we are doing the right thing by sheer willpower. But we should not conclude from this that we are doing the right thing only by our own strength and not by God's grace. Sometimes we think that God's grace is at work only when we *feel* it. But this is not true. Even when we do not feel the presence of God's grace in the soul, it can be there. It can be at work in the nonfeeling part of the soul — that is, in the thinking part or the mind, which is where the will operates. And this indeed is what happens when we do the right thing by using our willpower without the support of the emotion of liking. God's grace is powering the will to do the right thing, but in a way that is not felt in the feeling part of the soul.

Nonetheless, the ideal is to have the feeling part of the soul support the will. In other words, as much as possible, we want the emotions to support the will as it tries, under the direction of the mind, to do the right thing. This is why liking God is valuable. The emotion of liking God facilitates our ability to do the right thing, as God wants. We saw this in the case of prayer: Liking God makes it easier to overcome whatever disliking of prayer we are experiencing. And the same is true with other good actions done for God's sake. The more we like God, the more our emotions help our wills in doing the good action.

We are speaking here about the goal of integration that was mentioned in the introduction. The goal is that our emotions work with our minds in doing the things that lead us to God. When we love with the will, this is an exercise of the mind, or the thinking part of the soul. We see with our minds what is good and right, and we then will it. Thus, with respect to God, we see with our minds that He is our salvation, the One in whom all things will be well for us. In Him, nothing will be wanting, for He is the fullness of life. He is infinite goodness, wisdom, justice, beauty, and truth. In Him, all sorrows and injustices will be done away with. And in Him, we will have a joy beyond telling, far better than anything on earth. We know this with our minds, and so we love God with our wills. In other words, we *will* God — we *want* God.

But what we know and believe about God with our minds does not always resonate with the feeling part of our souls. Our minds know that nothing is more agreeable to our well-being than God. Yet, for various reasons, there are times when this perception of God as most agreeable does not seep down into the feeling part of our souls. The feeling or emotional part remains unmoved, unconvinced. So, there is no emotional liking for God. Then our wills must carry on without the support of our emotions.

Learning to Like God More Deeply

How, then, do we get what our minds know about God to seep down into the feeling part of our souls so that we will have an emotional liking for God that works with our wills? Without claiming that this is an exhaustive list, here are three valuable ways: prayer, upright living, and using creatures to think about God.

The first way of learning to like God more is by persevering in prayer. It has been said that God is an acquired taste, and Scripture says, "Taste and see that the LORD is good" (Ps 34:8). By tasting how good God is, we come to perceive more and more how agreeable He is. We acquire a taste for God. This happens especially in prayer. During prayer, we come to find God more and more agreeable to the deepest parts within us. In turn, we develop an emotional love for God.

I once heard the Catholic speaker and organizational expert Patrick Lencioni recount the following experience of praying the Rosary. He noted that he has a personal commitment to pray the Rosary every day but often he finds that, when the time comes to do so, it is hard to start. He wants to do other things instead.

Yet he pushes through reluctantly and begins to pray the Rosary. Then, after about five minutes, he thinks, "This is great! I should do this more often!" So, at first, he disliked praying the Rosary, and then he came to like it. What happened was that within prayer, he tasted the goodness of the Lord, and this kindled in him a liking for God that made him want to pray. It is not that our time in prayer will always lead to an emotional liking for God, but it often does, so this is one way we learn to like God.

Another way to cultivate our liking for God is by living uprightly. An upright life is a life lived according to God's will. By obeying God's ways, we walk with God and stay in His presence. In turn, His presence brings a profound peace and joy. This is experienced principally in the mind or thinking part of the soul. As the mind and will adhere to God by doing His will, they know a deep peace even in the midst of hardships. And, in turn, this experience of peace in the thinking part of the soul then touches the feeling part. After all, the two parts are not strangers but cohabitants of the same soul. They are constantly interacting with and affecting each other. So, as the thinking part experiences God's peace within itself, the feeling part senses that peace in the thinking part.

Of course, God is spiritual, and He cannot be felt. He is beyond the senses. Yet His peace in the thinking part of the soul can be felt by the feeling part. In this way, the feeling part tastes the goodness of God; it perceives His agreeableness as mediated through the thinking part of the soul. Saints have spoken of this as an "overflow" from the mind into the emotions. By a kind of osmosis, the mind's experience of God's agreeableness seeps into the feeling part of the soul, and the emotion of liking God arises. In heaven, this overflow will be to the fullest extent possible so the emotions will be fully alive with the love of God. But here on earth, it happens to a partial extent as we follow God's ways and live uprightly. And even though this overflow is only partial in this life, it is still valuable for getting us to like God.

As with tasting God's goodness in prayer, so here, too, it is not guaranteed that living uprightly will lead to an emotional liking for God. We may be living an upright life, but still, God in His providence wants us to experience a period of dryness. The period of dryness requires us to persevere in loving God with our will without the support of liking Him. In this way, the dryness helps us to remember that loving God with the will is more important than emotionally liking Him and that the will's love must take the lead over the emotion of love. But this overflow often does happen to some extent, and so upright living is one way in which we cultivate a liking for God.

A third way of learning to like God more is by using the good things in creation to think about God's goodness. The goodness we find in creatures reflects the divine goodness. For example, when we see a beautiful sunset, we praise God and realize that the beauty in the sunset is a reflection of God's beauty. But it is only a partial, limited reflection of His beauty. We realize that God is even more beautiful; indeed, He is infinite beauty itself.

In his *Summa Theologiae*, St. Thomas Aquinas helps us to see that there are three steps in this way of raising the mind to think about God in His infinite goodness. First, we see a likeness of God in something created. Then we realize that this likeness falls short of God's perfection. And so, third, we think of God as possessing the perfection in an infinite way. For another example, consider the love of a friend. That love is a likeness of God's love. But as great as that friend's love might be, it falls short of the divine love. So, we think of God as possessing the fullness of love, as infinite love itself.

This three-step process — or "triple way," as it is sometimes called — leads us to think about God in His infinite majesty, far above creation, and yet this way of thinking about God is built on what we observe in the world around us. We lift the mind all the way to God above the heavens, but we do so by looking at the likeness of God here on earth. Perhaps because of this humble grounding in creation, this way of thinking about God resonates with the feeling part of the soul and, in turn, it gives rise to and fosters an emotional liking for God.

The created thing that most of all lifts the mind to God and fosters an emotional liking for Him is the humanity of Jesus Christ. In His human nature, Jesus is a creature, a fellow human being. In His divine nature, He is God together with the Father and the Holy Spirit. Since His human nature is marvelously united with His divine nature in His divine Person, we find in His human nature the best possible created likenesses of the divine nature. We find not only the love of a friend, the justice of an upright man, and the wisdom of an intelligent person, but we find them to the fullest extent possible in a creature. So, when we observe the good things in Jesus' human nature, they most especially lead us to think of the divine majesty. Our minds are lifted up to think of the infinite love, the infinite justice, the infinite wisdom, and the other infinite perfections that are in God. This is why we should pay attention to the human life of Jesus and meditate on His humanity, since this will most of all foster an emotion of liking for God.

Keeping Our Love Elevated

Now, once we have the emotion of liking for God, we need to keep it pure, for it can degenerate. It degenerates when we love the consolations of God rather than the God of consolations, to use the turn of phrase attributed to St. Teresa of Ávila. The good things that we have and that comfort us are consolations that God gives us in our weakness. They are the created things we find agreeable and we like, including the things that can lift our minds to God, such as the beautiful sunset, the love of a friend, and the humanity of Jesus Christ. God gives us these things in order to sustain us and to encourage us on the journey to Him. But just as one can end up loving a gift more than its giver, we can end up liking these consolations more than God himself.

When this happens, the emotion of liking is drawn to the consolations as though they were ends in themselves. We end up liking them in a greedy, possessive way. The emotion of liking sees these consolations as the things in which we can find our rest and lasting joy rather than seeing God as the one in whom we find these things. And since the emotion of liking and the will's act of loving mutually influence each other, the emotion of liking then works on the will. The emotion of liking draws the will away from loving God for His own sake and leads it to seek its rest in the consolations rather than in God. Of course, we must resist this and use our wills to guide the emotion of liking back to God. Again, the will can direct the emotion of liking to God through prayer, upright living, and using creatures to think of God, most of all through reflecting on the humanity of Jesus Christ.

In fact, the humanity of Christ once again proves most helpful here. To see this, we turn to a beautiful teaching in St. Bernard of Clairvaux's sermons on the Ascension. Building on themes in the patristic era before him, he shows how the mysteries in the life of Christ help the emotion of liking to be lifted to God above. Saint Bernard highlights two mysteries of Jesus, in particular: the Incarnation and the Ascension.

Thanks to the Incarnation, God comes before us in human flesh. We like that. We find the humanity of Christ agreeable to our own human nature, and thus we love with an emotional love Jesus as a fellow human being. Indeed, the presence of God with us as a human being is the greatest consolation we have. Yet we need to love Jesus not only as a fellow human being, but also as God. We need to direct our will and also the emotion of love all the way up to the divine majesty itself.

To do this, Christ first gets us to like Him as a human being. Again, we find the humanity of Jesus agreeable to us. Or, as Saint Bernard puts it, we find the humanity of Jesus sweet. And since we find it sweet, we like it. Yet other sweet things compete with the humanity of Christ for our attention. Our attachment to these other sweet things does not help our salvation. Instead, our preoccupation with them leads us astray. So, in order to save us, God has to wrest our attention from these sweet things. He does so by sending us another sweet thing in their place: He gives us the sweetness of the Incarnation to replace the sweetness of these other things.

Saint Bernard elsewhere has a great line about this, alluding to a woodworking trick. In his Sermon 20 on the Song of Songs, he writes: "Sweetness conquers sweetness as one nail drives out another." When a nail is stuck in a piece of wood, you can use another nail to drive it out. Just so, the sweetness of Jesus' humanity drives out our attachment to other sweet things.

But the ultimate aim is not simply to like Jesus' humanity; it is to like His divinity. Yet through liking His humanity, we are led to like His divinity. Getting our attention fixed on His human nature, the Lord then draws our sights upward, so that we come to love and like Him in His divine nature. Here is where the mystery of the Ascension comes in. God especially draws our attention upward through the Ascension. As Christ's humanity is lifted up out of this world to the right hand of the Father, our love is lifted up and directed beyond all creation to God himself.

God is training us to like Him in His wonderful divinity. Through the humanity of Jesus, God raises not only our wills but also our emotional love so that it has His divine majesty as its object. We taste and see that He is good, that He is most agreeable in His divinity. We therefore convert — that is, turn — our emotion of liking to nothing short of God.

Conclusion

When our emotion of liking is lifted up to God himself, then, by God's grace, we have done an important work in converting our emotions. We have repaired the foundation on which all the other emotions are built. Also, to the extent that this is done, that concrete love of God that is a composite of both the will and the emotion of liking is less divided. The will no longer works in one direction and the emotion of liking in another. Instead, we love God and all other things for God's sake (especially other people for His sake) with a more wholehearted love, as we should.

....

Glory be to the Father and to the Son and to the Holy Spirit; as it was in the beginning, is now, and ever shall be, world without end. Amen.

CHAPTER 3
Resolve and Hope

In my studies, I have noticed a word frequently occurring in
ancient monastic texts. In Greek, the word is *próthesis*; in Latin, it is *propositus*. This word has been translated in different
ways, but we can call it "resolve." In these monastic writings, the
authors urge monks to keep their resolve, the resolve they had
when they first joined the monastery, the resolve, as the *Rule of
Saint Benedict* expresses it, to take up "the strong and noble weap-
ons of obedience to do battle for the true King, Christ the Lord."

These authors knew that monks can lose their resolve. Their
determination to follow Christ wholeheartedly, no matter what
the sacrifice, can slacken. They can lose their vigor, their ardor,

their love. Saint Benedict tells his monks that they are to place nothing before the love of Christ, but experience shows that monks can put other loves first. At least, I have found this to be so with myself.

But isn't this a problem for every vocation? When we first accept some calling, we are often eager and zealous for the work before us. This happens whether the calling is a lifelong vocation, such as to marriage or to religious life, or a temporary calling to do some work, such as to volunteer as a teacher in the parish's religious education program. At first, we like the work we have been called to do; we think of the good that we can do through it, and so we have fervor. But over time, we lose that first fervor. Whether for monk or married person, for parish priest or volunteer, the loss of one's resolve is a common problem.

Think, too, of the vocation we all share: the vocation to be a Christian. We entered this most important and foundational calling when we were baptized. For those of us who were baptized as children, we did not initially have the fervor and the resolve that I have been speaking about. But if we have remained disciples of Christ in the years after our baptism, then there have likely been times when we were on fire for our Christian vocation. We saw it as a great gift, and we were resolved to live it out well. Still, over time, as the years wash over us, our fervor and resolve can fade away.

So, when these ancient authors urge monks to keep their determination, we can hear them telling all of us to do the same. Stay resolved! God has called us to follow Him, to embark on a journey that leads to Him and His kingdom. What is more, we are closer now than when we first began (see Rom 13:11)! So we must not let our love grow cold (Mt 24:13; Gal 6:9–10; Rv 2:4–5; 3:15–16) but must keep on working on conversion through Jesus Christ. And to persevere in this way on the journey to God's kingdom, we need resolve.

In the first chapter, I spoke about fear and the real danger that we will stray from the path that leads to God. Losing our resolve is another way we can stray from that path. As noted, the ancient monastic literature is especially mindful of this danger. Thus, the monastic author St. John Cassian, in his *Conferences*, warns monks against becoming lukewarm, for that is what we become when we lose our resolve. Saint Athanasius, in the opening of his famous biography of the model monk, Saint Antony, repeats the word for *resolve* a few times and emphasizes the example of Saint Antony's resolve. This suggests that a lack of resolve was something of a problem among the monks to whom Saint Athanasius was writing. But again, this is not a problem only for monks.

Resolve Is Based on What We Desire

Being resolved presupposes that you want something. To put this in the terms we used in the last chapter, you like something, and not yet having it, you desire it. So, to reflect on monastic resolve, I want to start by speaking about what we desire. Resolve is very much an exercise in desire. If we are to keep our resolve strong, we must keep alive our desire.

The Catholic tradition gives us a way to think about what we desire and are willing to work for. It does so by speaking of three ways of serving God: as a slave, as a mercenary, or as a son or a child. Each of these serves, but they are different in what they desire to attain by their service. The slave serves God in order to avoid punishment. The mercenary serves God in order to attain a reward other than God. And the child serves God in order to attain God — that is, to be one with God.

So, the service of the slave springs from a sort of negative desire. He or she desires to avoid the pains of punishment. The slave may be taken here to represent those who desire to protect what they have and not lose it. Such people are fine with the status quo; they desire not to have more but to protect what they do have. So, the slave's desire is not for God himself. It is not even concerned with attaining more than he currently has.

This is similar to the bad servant in the parable of the talents (see Mt 25:14–30). He buries what he has in order not to lose it. Clearly, this won't do for those who are on a journey. Being on a journey means that you are not content as you are, but instead, you desire more and, in turn, work to attain more. And since we are on a journey to God, we are to desire and work to attain nothing short of God.

How about the mercenary? Well, the mercenary has the desire to attain more. Not content with what he has, he seeks more, and he is willing to work for it. But the problem is that the extra things that he wants fall short of God. Yes, he desires more good things than he currently has, but they are all in the realm of created things. He is not desirous of God himself. His sights are not upon God, who far surpasses all created goods, no matter how great those goods are.

Maybe the created goods that the mercenary wants are things that bring pleasure, prestige, power, or wealth. But other possibilities are goods of the soul, such as the virtues. Is it wrong to desire virtues as one's reward? Actually, it depends. If we are seeking them as the final end in our journey, then our desire is, in fact, wrong. Saint Augustine is strong on this point. Our souls should ultimately desire the attainment of God and nothing short of God. We should want the virtues and work for them, but they are meant to bring us to God. If we try to have the virtues without also having God, then we are left clinging to our virtues and not to God. Saint Augustine says that the virtues then become sham virtues, not real ones.

So, the mercenary is better than the slave because he desires more than he already has. But the mercenary is wrong to let his desire rest simply on attaining created goods, whether he desires physical goods or even goods of the soul.

The child represents the ideal. The child desires nothing short of God, and so the child is resolved to do what is needed to attain God. This is the desire that we should have: a desire for God himself. We are called to this as Christians. What Saint Benedict tells his monks applies to all Christians: We are to seek God truly — nothing less than that. The end of the journey is full union with God — nothing short of that. So, our desire should stretch all the way to God.

We can — and should — examine ourselves on this point: "Where is my desire? Has it come to rest on the status quo? Have I become complacent? Or, like the mercenary, have I come to desire a reward that is other than God? Does my desire reach to God? Where is my desire?"

If we find that our desire is falling short of God, this suggests that our love is not ultimately for God but has fallen from God to created things — a problem I spoke about and gave remedies for at the end of the previous chapter. We might say that when we have to labor for God, that provides a test of how true our love for God is — that is, a test of whether our wills and the emotion of liking are directed all the way to God himself.

The Emotion of Hope

Again, our liking for God and, in turn, our desire for God, are at the heart of monastic resolve. But resolve entails more than liking and desiring. Some things we like and desire and then obtain without much ado. For example, I like coffee, and when I desire it, all that I need to do is go to the coffeepot and get some. I then enjoy coffee. It's not difficult but is straightforward. Yet our journey to God is different. It is difficult. After all, it is the difficulty of obtaining God that makes it necessary to have resolve.

The difficulty in the endeavor brings into play another very important emotion: the emotion of hope. In the rest of this chapter, we will reflect on the emotion of hope. Obviously, to hope for something means that we like it and desire it. But there's more. First, we like and desire something — that is, we want something. But the additional feature in cases of hope is this: There is something between us and what we want. There is some distance, some obstacle, some difficulty that needs to be overcome in order to get the thing we want. That's the situation in which hope occurs: Something stands between us and what we want.

This raises the question: Can that obstacle be overcome in order to attain what we desire? If we see the obstacle as insurmountable, we have not hope but the emotion of despair. Yet if we perceive that the obstacle can be overcome, then we have the emotion of hope. That's the perception at the basis of hope: It is the perception that what stands between me and what I want can be overcome. If I have that perception, I have hope.

For example, suppose I am a young person who wants to become a medical doctor. What stands between me and that goal? Much schoolwork, getting into medical school, learning all that needs to be learned in medical school, and securing student loans, to say nothing of paying them off. If I think that all these difficulties can be overcome, I have hope. But if I think they cannot be overcome, I have despair.

In our lifelong journey as Christians, what we want is God; we are resolved upon attaining God. The difficulties that stand between us and the attainment of God are many. We encounter many obstacles on the road of conversion that leads to God. If we see these as able to be overcome, we have hope. But if we don't believe they can be overcome, we have despair. The difference is in how we perceive the obstacles in our way.

To make this more practical, we can break it down into smaller bits, as it were. The hope that we have is for God. We hope to attain full and perfect union with God. But this is not attained all at once. There is a gradual, step-by-step process of growing closer to God in our everyday lives. So, what we ultimately want and hope for is full union with God. But more proximately, what we want is to come closer to God — even if only a little bit each day.

We can thus think of hope more incrementally. There is the hope for full union with God, and then there is the smaller hope of making a little more progress toward God today or in a particular moment or over some period of time. We have this hope, for example, at the beginning of Lent. We hope to make progress and to grow closer to God during that holy season.

Even in these smaller instances of hope, where the object is to come closer to God, there are obstacles. And it is here that hope is concretely practiced: when I face an obstacle that stands between me and the next step of conversion. In that situation, the question arises: "Do I believe that this difficulty can be overcome, in order to take the next step in my conversion?" How I answer this determines whether I have the emotion of hope.

There are many such difficulties between us and further conversion. When I first joined the monastery, I remember the difficulty I encountered was the quiet evenings. I had been used to hanging out with friends or family in the evening. But in the monastery, I was alone, and it was quiet. Silence is something monks observe for the sake of monastic conversion, but I found it difficult at first.

There are parallels in other vocations. For example, when a husband and a wife begin their lives together, there are adjustments to be made, and they can prove difficult. An example might be something as mundane as sharing a common bed. One spouse snores or moves a lot in his or her sleep, and this deprives the other of sleep. Or think of the vocation of parenthood. When a child comes along, so much changes! Before this, the parents could come and go as they pleased, but when a child arrives, the child needs to be watched and cared for all the time.

Whatever your vocation or situation, to take the next step on the journey of conversion, you must do the things that contribute to your conversion — things such as fulfilling your duties (whether as a monk, spouse, parent, or otherwise) and practicing virtues, such as charity, prudence, and patience. But when you find those duties hard to do or you are cranky so that it is hard to be virtuous, then you are encountering a difficulty that stands between you and the next step in your ongoing conversion. Do you think the difficulty can be overcome? Again, your answer to that will determine whether you have the emotion of hope.

And this applies not only to those difficulties that we encounter at the beginning of a vocation. Over time, the initial difficulties may go away, but others follow. That is, the difficulties that stand as obstacles to further conversion change over time. Consider some examples from the monastic vocation. At times, the difficulty may be the vow of obedience, when I am told to do something I don't want to do. Or the challenge at some point may be with celibacy. Often it is patience with one's fellow monks or one's superiors or with one's community in general. Sometimes the difficulty concerns the work one has to do: I have a lot of work to do, so I find it hard to practice balance. Ongoing conversion requires that I achieve greater balance, but that's difficult. Sometimes the difficulty is giving up something; at other times, it is the difficulty of taking on something new.

These difficulties in monastic life are not all that different from those faced by people in any vocation. Those who are not monks face difficulties with obeying bosses at work or obeying the wishes of a spouse, with being chaste according to one's state in life, with practicing patience toward others, with creating work-life balance, with giving up something, and with taking on something new.

Another kind of difficulty we all might face is illness or the limitations of old age. We are called to patient endurance when we face these, but it is hard! A few decades ago, a monk from my monastic community became the archbishop of Dubuque, Iowa. After he retired, illness and old age slowed him down, and he found this very difficult. He did not handle it well at first. But he had a sort of conversion eventually, and he even wrote a piece in the archdiocesan newspaper apologizing for how difficult he had been to deal with when he first ran into the difficulties of old age. Accepting his newfound limitations with patience was the difficulty that stood between him and ongoing conversion at the time.

What stands between us and the next step in our ongoing conversion will change at different points in our lives. But as Christians, we have to be very clear that there will be difficulties, as Saint Benedict reminds his monks. He says: "The novice should be clearly told all the hardships and difficulties that will lead him to God." The Latin more literally says that *through* these hardships and difficulties the novice goes to God. These "hardships and difficulties" therefore stand between us and coming closer to God through the next step in conversion. We must pass through them, work through them, in order to journey closer to God.

Again, the emotion of hope has to do with how I perceive the difficulty that stands between me and further conversion. I have hope when I perceive that difficulty to be something that can be overcome. But if I perceive it as impossible to overcome, I do not have hope; instead, I have despair.

Here's another worthwhile set of questions for self-examination: "What difficulties stand between me and conversion? What's keeping me from coming closer to God? What difficult thing must I do or endure, or do or endure better, in order to grow in virtue and come closer to God?"

After we have identified a difficulty that stands between us and ongoing conversion, we can ask: "Do I think this difficulty can be overcome? What steps can I take — even if small steps —

to make progress in working through this difficulty?" If I see that the difficulty can be overcome, then there arises the emotion of hope, which helps me to stay resolved. But if not, then again, there is despair, even if a quiet despair.

I suspect that there are many cases of quiet despair among Christians. We have run into difficulties; this conversion thing is harder than we expected, and in turn, we have lost hope in the possibility of continual conversion. Yet if we despair of growing closer to God in some particular area, then we give up trying. Our resolve weakens.

So, we want to keep hope alive. We need hope in order to keep our resolve strong. Don't be discouraged when you find conversion difficult and painful. Yes, these difficulties remind us that there is still a distance between us and perfect union with God. In other words, we are not there yet; we have not yet reached the final destination on our journey. But that is not a reason to lose hope.

In fact, hope does not entail thinking that we have reached perfection; instead, it entails thinking that we *can* reach perfection *eventually*. Hope is not for those who have arrived at perfect union with God but for those who have not yet arrived there. Hope is for all of us who are still struggling with conversion.

Putting Our Hope in God

Thus far, I have been speaking of the emotion of hope. But we can also speak of making an act of hope with our will. When we make an act of hope with our will, we see with our mind and decide with our will that the obstacle can be overcome. Sometimes we must make this decision even though we do not have the emotion of hope. In such cases, we are hoping against hope. We hope through an act of the will, even though we do not have hope as an emotion.

But as I have said repeatedly, we are trying to get the thinking part of the soul and the feeling part of the soul to work to-gether. So, we want to cultivate the emotion of hope to go along with and to support the will's act of hoping.

Again, the emotion of hope depends on perceiving that the difficult work of conversion can be successfully done. We perceive that the obstacles in the way of making progress in conversion can be overcome. Yet we cannot overcome the obstacles by ourselves, but only with God. Maybe, then, we need to renew our trust and confidence in God's grace. Renewing this trust and confidence is something we need to do now and again.

People have sometimes noted the distinction between what we hope *in* and what we hope *for*. What we hope *in* is what will enable us to overcome the obstacle standing between us and what we want. God's grace is therefore what we hope in; it is what will enable us to overcome the obstacles to closer union with God. Scripture, therefore, exhorts us not to put our hope in other things, such as human beings, whether ourselves or others, or in "horses," that is, in worldly power (see Ps 146:3; Jer 17:5; Is 31:1). Instead, we are to put our hope in God's assistance, an assistance that is offered to us through faith in the humanity of Jesus Christ.

God's help is strong enough to overcome any obstacle, for He can do all things, even forgive our sins, no matter how great. And God in His love wants to help us, for as Jesus says to the leper in the Gospel, "I am willing. ... Be clean" (Mk 1:41, NIV).

So, let us hope in God's help, in His grace. That is what we hope *in*. Another way of saying this is that we hope in God's mercy. His grace is given to us out of His mercy, not our deserving it. As Saint Benedict says in his *Rule*, we must never lose hope in God's mercy. Saint Augustine says something similar in his *Confessions*: "All my hope is found solely in your exceeding great mercy."

We hope *in* God's mercy. What we hope *for* is the attainment of God. But since the perfect attainment of God will come only in the future, what we hope for in the present is to make more progress — even if merely a little more progress — on the journey of conversion and thus to come closer to God. If we renew our hope in and for God, then this will strengthen our resolve to continue the work of ongoing conversion.

To conclude, I want to share the story of a saint who shows us what it means not to lose hope in God's mercy. I came across this saint when I was a novice at my monastery. Back then, I got into the practice of reading the lives of the saints. Each morning, before my work assignment began, I'd read about some of the saints for the day from the old version of *Butler's Lives of the Saints.*

One day, I read about the Vietnamese martyrs, including Bl. Thomas Toan. Blessed Thomas was a layman and a catechist, and when the rulers in Vietnam cracked down on the Church there in the nineteenth century, he was rounded up. He was tortured, and under the torture, he rejected Christ. But after he was released, he repented and began again to profess faith in Christ. So, he was again brought in and tortured. Again, he renounced his faith and was released. But again, he repented and professed faith in Christ. A third time he was arrested and tortured, but this time he did not deny Christ. Instead, he persevered through the cruel torture and became a martyr of Jesus Christ.

What inspires me about Bl. Thomas Toan is not simply his martyrdom, but that he did not give up after his failures. I would be tempted to despair after failing to profess Christ, if not the first time, then the second time. I'd be tempted to think, "There is no hope. I am unable to remain true to Christ when put to the test." But Blessed Thomas did not despair. After failing, he renewed his resolve to follow Christ faithfully and put his hope in God.

The difficulty that stands between us and becoming closer to God is probably not as great as imprisonment and torture. But still, it might be a great difficulty. Sometimes the challenges that we encounter in the work of conversion are hidden and yet very big. In the end — that is, in heaven — we will see the "hardships and difficulties" through which people journeyed toward God, and I think we will be surprised at how great some of them were for people we never suspected had them. Whatever our hardship, we put our hope in God that He will give us the strength to persevere and to attain the prize of our upward calling in Christ (see Phil 3:14).

....

Glory be to the Father and to the Son and to the Holy Spirit;
as it was in the beginning, is now, and ever shall be, world
without end. Amen.

CHAPTER 4
Problems with Anger

In this chapter, I want to speak about anger. I have spoken of the emotions of fear, love, desire, and hope. And I have tried to show how these can help us in our journey to the kingdom of God. But with the emotion of anger, I will mostly consider how it hurts us. I will say some things about when anger is good, but for the most part, I will speak about it as a hindrance. Anger is one of the things that can especially get in the way of conversion; indeed, it can be spiritually deadly. And unfortunately, it is fairly common in our lives.

Here are some quotes to show how destructive anger can be to conversion. St. John Cassian writes in his *Conferences*, "What one gains from fasting will not balance out what one loses from anger, nor is the profit from reading so great as the harm which results from despising a brother." And then there is the Lord himself, when He teaches: "You have heard that it was said to the men of old, 'You shall not kill; and whoever kills shall be liable to judgment.' But I say to you that every one who is angry with his brother shall be liable to judgment; whoever insults his brother shall be liable to the council, and whoever says, 'You fool' shall be liable to the hell of fire" (Mt 5:21–22).

Strong words about anger! We must overcome bad forms of anger, which thwart our journey to God.

The Difficulty with Controlling Anger

When we consider times when the emotion of anger arises, the first thing to note is our lack of control over when it arises. As noted in the introduction, emotions can be unwieldy things. We do not *directly* control whether they arise within us, and this is especially the case with the emotion of anger.

As you might recall if you ever took an ethics class, Aristotle put it this way: He said that we cannot rule over the emotions in a *despotic* way. The despot simply tells subjects what to do, and they do it. But that does not work with the emotions. We can tell ourselves not to have an emotion, but that doesn't mean it will go away. So, we might be afraid of something and, although we keep telling ourselves not to be afraid of it, the fear continues. (Recall my ghost story in the first chapter.) Or we can tell ourselves not to have hope, but still we have it. This happens with sports fans. Their team is doing well, so they start hoping for a championship. But they don't want to get their hopes up, and they tell themselves not to hope for a championship, for they have been disappointed before. Yet sometimes they can't help it — they hope for the championship nonetheless.

This especially happens with anger. You tell yourself not to be angry, but it doesn't matter. The anger does not go away.

So, we don't rule over our emotions in a despotic way, in which we can tell our emotions to stop and they do so. Aristotle says that, instead, we rule over the emotions in a *political* way. Here, *political* refers to the Greek *polis* or city, where persons are not subjects but free citizens. To rule them, one needs to persuade them. So, too, with the emotions: We need to persuade them to react in the ways we want. We will speak more about this in chapter 8.

While we cannot always control whether anger stirs within us, what we can control is how we deal with its stirrings. For instance, do we go along with the promptings of anger or resist them? If our anger is unjust or excessive, we have a responsibility to resist its promptings.

This is the teaching of early Christian writers, such as Origen. It's a humane teaching, telling us not to be upset or to feel defeated when we have unwanted emotions. After all, we cannot directly control whether we have them. Rather than be upset or feel defeated, we can direct our energy toward resisting the bad urgings of these emotions. Yes, it is not nice having these unwanted emotions. It can feel as if we are on a battlefield and are being bombarded by their bad urgings. But we need not fret, for Christ is with us in the fight; we should not feel defeated, for the battle is not over. In many respects, the battle has just begun. When the unwanted emotion arises, that is when the fight against it begins, and in Christ we can attain the victory.

The Perception behind Anger

While we cannot *directly* control whether we have the emotion of anger, we can learn to manage it. What is especially helpful is to look at the perception that gives rise to anger. As I have said, all emotions stem from perceptions, and anger is no exception. What, then, is the perception behind anger? It is the perception of an injustice. The emotion of anger is a response to a perceived injustice. By understanding this, we can better manage our anger.

With anger, one perceives that something happened that should *not* have happened. What happened, whether recently or in the past, is seen to be not only undesirable but also unfair, unjust, or somehow wrong and undeserved. Having perceived such an injustice, one responds with anger — an anger that protests, resists, fights, or tries to overcome the wrong that happened. This is the good purpose of anger: It gives a person the energy to protest an injustice, rather than to be content with it, and so to work, when possible, to correct that injustice.

Again, at the root of anger as an emotion is the perception of an injustice. To give some examples, the injustice could be that someone was cheated out of money, or that someone's reputation was wrongly maligned, or that someone was treated disrespectfully. But the injustice need only be *perceived* for anger to arise. It need not be real. A jealous husband might perceive the injustice of infidelity where it does not exist, and as a result, the husband gets angry, even though there has been no infidelity by his wife.

Smoke is said to be a sign of fire, but when anger rages, it is not a sure sign that there has, in fact, been an injustice. It is only a sign that someone has *perceived* an injustice. So, sometimes there is anger where no wrong has been committed.

We can think of people who are likely to perceive a wrong even when there is none. I mentioned already a jealous husband. Also, someone who has been wronged in the past can be especially prone to perceive injustice. Such a person has been fooled once and is therefore on guard not to be fooled again. By perceiving an injustice even when it is not there, such people become angry without a legitimate cause.

This also happens to people who are under a lot of stress. They readily perceive an injustice or wrong even though there is none. They are therefore quick to anger. It is interesting that in chapter 64 of his *Rule*, Saint Benedict counsels the abbot not to be agitated or excitable. Saint Benedict knows that the abbot, as the head of the monastery, is often under a lot of stress!

In the popular 1946 movie *It's a Wonderful Life*, there is a scene that portrays how easily a stressed-out person sees wrongs that are not there and then gets angry. The hero in the movie, George Bailey, comes upon hard times. He's in dire straits and thus under tremendous stress. So, when he returns home at the end of the day, he gets angry at everyone and everything.

He learns that his daughter caught a cold coming home from school, and he gets angry at the teacher for not making his daughter button up her coat before leaving school. Another daughter is practicing the piano, and he gets angry at her for making noise. One of his sons asks him for help on a project, and he gets angry at him too, as if his son were wrong to ask for help. George even gets angry at the knob on the banister when it comes loose. It is as if he thinks the knob did something wrong! It's probably a sign that unjustified anger has a grip on someone when that person starts getting angry at inanimate objects.

The Vice of Anger

The point is that we can get angry when we shouldn't. The wrong or injustice that gives rise to our anger is only perceived and not real; it does not truly exist. Such cases of anger are obviously not good. They are based not in reality but in errant perceptions.

Again, stressed-out people and people who have been wronged in the past are prone to see injustices even when they are not there. Another thing that makes people prone to see injustices that are not real is the vice of anger.

Vices are like virtues, in that they are abiding tendencies to act in a certain way. A virtue is an abiding disposition to do a kind of act that is good for oneself — that is, good for one's true fulfillment. A vice is an abiding disposition to do a kind of act that is bad for oneself — that is, does not contribute to but frustrates one's fulfillment.

So, the vice of anger is present when I have developed a tendency to be angry in a bad way. Getting angry in a bad way has become ingrained, habitual. I'm prone to do it. But we need not have this vice within us to get angry now and again. We can succumb to an instance of anger, whether or not we have the vice of anger. But when we have this vice, we are prone to see injustices where there are none and to become angry without a legitimate cause.

With the vice of anger, we often get mad at this or that person, or perhaps even at everyone. We see wrongs, faults, injustices all around us — even though they are not truly there. We think this person should not have done such and such, or that person should have done something that he did not do. We don't like how that person laughed. Or we are bothered because so-and-so did not say something we thought she should have said. Or we are mad because the person ahead of us in the checkout line is going too slowly, and that means a whole two minutes in our lives has been wasted. With the vice of anger, we can get angry at the smallest or even stupidest of things.

With the vice of anger, I tend to like people when they agree with me, but I do not like them otherwise. If I am an angry person, in fact, I tend to divide the world into two camps: those people whom I like and those who annoy me. There is a sort of lingering anger toward the latter group — the annoying people — for I consider it wrong that they do not do as I like. Indeed, as the vice of anger burrows deeper into my heart, the group of people who annoy me, and toward whom I have a lingering anger, grows in number. Meanwhile, the circle of people whom I find acceptable shrinks.

The saints have said that all virtues contribute to charity, which is the greatest virtue. On the other hand, all vices are rooted in pride, which is the greatest vice. Saint Augustine teaches that when we have true love, all things are directed to the attainment of God. But when we have pride, all things are referred to oneself. God is not the center, but I become the center. In this way, the proud person is self-centered.

Now, if all the vices are rooted in pride, this means that the vice of anger is also rooted in pride. And given that pride is about self-centeredness, anger will display a kind of self-centeredness. It surely does. The person with the vice of anger suffers from being self-centered.

Notice that a self-centered person thinks that things should serve *his* desires and wants. Thus, when things do not go that person's way or when people do not think as that person thinks, this in itself is considered a wrong. It is perceived as something that should not happen, and thus the self-centered person gets mad.

Consider the following story. I witnessed this when I was residing in another religious community. One day, I was at lunch in the community's dining area. There were about forty men living in the community. One of them sat down next to me and complained about the egg salad on his plate. He said with frustration, "I don't understand it. I've told them again and again how my mom made egg salad. But the kitchen still does not make it the right way!" For him, his mom's way of making egg salad was the right way. It was the way he liked it. So, in his mind, the kitchen was doing something wrong by making egg salad differently.

This religious was apparently unmindful of the fact that there were *thirty-nine other people* living in the community! All of them could point to how their moms, if not they themselves, made egg salad. Was the kitchen expected to accommodate all their preferences for making egg salad? Yet, due to self-centeredness, this religious could think only of the way he wanted egg salad made. Any other way was wrong and warranted his anger.

Whether it be food or something else, how easily we grumble about the way things are done, as if there were some *real* injustice, whereas, in reality, there is only a difference from how we want something done. The result is the unrighteous anger of the self-centered.

Now, this should not lead us to think, "That sure describes so-and-so!" Rather, we should remember that each of us is self-centered in some respects or at some moments. It is part of our fallen condition. It goes with pride and self-will. So, each of us should reflect on how we ourselves sometimes succumb to what may be called "the egg salad syndrome." Each of us should reflect on how we get angry over things when the only so-called injustice is that things do not go as we want.

When the Injustice Is Real

But what about cases when there really is an injustice to be angry about? Is it OK or even morally good to be angry then? I would say that such anger, arising from a real injustice, can be morally acceptable or even useful. Again, a good anger serves the purpose of protesting and perhaps also correcting a real injustice. Major authors in the monastic tradition, such as Evagrius and St. John Cassian, however, say that anger is good only when it is directed at our own vices and their tempting suggestions. It is never rightly directed outwardly toward others.

In thinking about anger, some Church Fathers considered Ephesians 4:26. A common translation is, "If you are angry, let it be without sin." Saint Paul is quoting a Greek translation of Psalm 4:4, which literally says, "Be angry and do not sin," rather than "If you are angry, let it be without sin." That is, this biblical verse in the Greek New Testament is exhorting us to be angry.

St. John Cassian interprets this as follows: "And so we are commanded to get angry in a healthy way, at ourselves and at the evil suggestions that make an appearance, and not to sin by letting them have a harmful effect." Cassian sees this verse as supporting his teaching that we are to be angry only against our own vices and their evil suggestions. Thus, the biblical texts tell us to be angry at temptations so that we resist them and do not sin.

In his *Confessions*, Saint Augustine also speaks about this verse. He says that it was the object of his meditation in the days soon after his conversion, while he was on retreat with friends in the village of Cassiciacum. He recounts, "Then I read, 'Be angry and sin not,' and how these words moved me, my God! I had already learned to feel for my past sins an anger with myself that would hold me back from sinning again.'" He goes on to say how he directs this anger inwardly, to fighting against and slaying the old nature, so as to live anew in God's light.

So, like Evagrius and Cassian, Augustine talks about anger as being good when directed toward the evil tendencies within us. These evil tendencies are unjust, they war against what is good and right in us, and they should not be there.

To be angry at the evil tendencies within me is not self-hatred, for I am not angry at anything that belongs to my true self. My true identity is a person made in the image of God and called to communion with Him through a holy life. The sinful tendencies within me do not belong to this true identity but work against it and threaten to obscure it. So I rightly perceive them as unjust and have anger toward them. That anger causes me to protest them and fight against them, and this helps me to avoid sinning.

It is like the zealous anger we would have toward someone's efforts to harm a loved one, such as a family member or a friend. Thus, when we love our true selves, we have anger toward the evil tendencies within us because they would harm our true selves and work against God's plans for us. This anger is not about self-hatred, but rather about a healthy self-love.

But can anger that is directed not at the sinful tendencies within oneself but at injustices outside oneself ever be morally good? What if I hear about the slaughter of innocent people —

can I have a good anger then? I think so. But the problem is that even this anger, which arises from a just cause, is very often not constructive. Even when our anger is based on a real injustice, it is often excessive and takes control over us. It is then wrong in that way.

Remember what the Letter of James says: "Know this, my beloved brethren. Let every man be quick to hear, slow to speak, slow to anger, for the anger of man does not work the righteousness of God" (1:19–20). So often our anger is excessive and does not lead to right action. Thus, it does not serve God's righteous ways.

The Need for Patience

There is a parallel here with the emotion of fear. I said in chapter 1 that there are two conditions for a good fear: The fear has to be based on a real danger, and its reaction to that danger cannot be excessive, such as by causing a person to freeze or to panic. Likewise with anger: A good anger has to be based on a real injustice, and its reaction to that injustice cannot be excessive. The common way for anger to be excessive is that it bulldozes our thinking so that we make poor decisions. If anger's protest against an injustice is to be used constructively, then right thinking, and not anger, needs to be in control of our actions.

So, on one hand, we cannot always control whether the emotion of anger arises in us, as we saw earlier in the chapter. But on the other hand, this does not mean we must be under the control of anger. We cannot always control when anger arises, but we can control whether we go along with its urgings. And yet, is that true? Can one always control whether one goes along with the urgings of anger? It would seem that in some cases, one cannot. There are people who cannot control themselves when they get angry. They let off harsh words or even start throwing things, if not doing something worse. Still, when I say that we *can* control whether we go along with the urgings of anger, that means that we *can develop* that control, even if we do not have it presently. With the help of God's grace, we can and should develop the ability not to be ruled by anger, but instead to stay in control of our actions.

A crucial virtue here is patience. Patience is an extremely important virtue with regard to anger, giving us the ability not to be controlled by our anger. It enables us to endure injustices without reacting in a knee-jerk, excessive, or uncontrolled way. Patience, in other words, gives us self-possession.

Saint Benedict speaks of patience when he describes the fourth of his twelve steps of humility:

> The fourth step of humility is when in this very obedi-
> ence, experiencing hard and adverse situations, or even
> when any injuries are inflicted, [the monk] embraces
> patient suffering with a quiet spirit and, bearing up, he
> does not grow weary nor walk away, for as Scripture
> says, "Whoever should persevere to the end, that person
> will be saved" (Mt 10:22); and again, "Let your heart be
> strong and be sustained by the Lord" (Ps 27:14).

Saint Benedict speaks of injuries being inflicted and of adverse situations. We can take these to be, at least sometimes, real injustices. So, here we have cases when anger arises from the perception of a wrong that is truly there. Saint Benedict says we should be able to embrace such situations with "patient suffering" and "with a quiet spirit" and "not grow weary nor walk away."

The reference to walking away is interesting, and I will say more about it in chapter 6. Now I want to note Saint Benedict's statement that we need to learn "patient suffering with a quiet spirit." When there is a real injustice and we suffer it patiently, we surely do feel the pain of it. Yet having a "quiet spirit," we do not react rashly and in a nonconstructive way. We endure the injustice with patience, and we are free, therefore, to think with sufficient clarity about how to deal with the injustice correctly.

In other words, patience enables us to keep our inner poise and stay in control, rather than to be ruled by the urgings of anger. And if this is important to do when the anger is based on a real injustice, then it is surely important to do when the anger is not based on a real injustice. That is, patience is needed both when the anger is justified and when it is not.

In fact, when anger arises, we do not always see clearly whether the anger is based on a real injustice. Anger can be so forceful that it carries us away, so we do not have the mental poise to tell whether we are perceiving a real injustice or only an imagined one.

Thus, when anger arises, not only must we maintain control over its urgings rather than be controlled by them, but we must also discern whether the anger is justified. The first — maintaining control — will be the more immediate task. Otherwise, we may do harm even if our anger is justified. But then we must also discern whether the anger *is* justified.

This shows us once again the importance of patience. The inner poise that patience gives is needed to do the first task of maintaining control over anger's urgings, and it is also needed for the second task. By preserving a quiet spirit within us, patience enables us both to stay in control of our anger and to discern whether there is a real injustice at the root of our anger.

Having patience in such cases does not mean that we do not feel the anger. Oh, it may be felt very much! We may still feel it simmering, if not rapidly boiling, within us. But with the self-possession that patience bestows, we keep the urgings of anger under control and we look at whether the perceived injustice is a real one.

Humility Also Needed

There is another virtue that is important here — namely, humility. When we try to discern whether we have a legitimate cause for anger, we will often have to deal with our pride. Recall that pride is marked by a self-centeredness that distorts our perception of things. It leads us to see something we dislike as an injustice simply because the thing goes against our wishes.

But it gets worse. This self-centeredness often cloaks itself in virtue. For example, suppose I do not like the taste of some food that is repeatedly served at my monastery. So, I get angry, and I complain about it. But to justify my anger I say that my concern is really with the health of the community. I say, "This food is not healthy, so it should not be served." In truth, I am angry because the food does not taste the way I like, but I pretend that it is really about the health of the community. "You see," I tell others and even myself, "I am really concerned with everyone's health."

Of course, when self-centeredness cloaks itself in some virtue, it is no more a virtue than a wolf in sheepskin is a sheep. And yet we can fool ourselves. The self-centeredness of pride is so pervasive that we even believe our own malarkey. This capacity for self-deception makes it even harder to discern whether there is a real injustice behind our anger.

Recall that this is already hard to discern due to the commotion caused within us by anger. Now it is even harder due to the self-deception that comes from pride. To work against the commotion within us, we need patience. It lessens the dustup within us caused by anger and maintains our mental poise. And to work against self-deception, we need humility.s It cuts through the pretenses of pride. Humility, that is, sees past the lies spoken in our self-centeredness so that we may more honestly assess whether our anger is justified.

Humility is sometimes tied to behavior and sometimes to thought. Here, I am tying it to how we think. In particular, humility concerns how I think about myself. Pride makes me have an overinflated view of myself so that I think everything revolves around me. Humility rejects this. It has a true and honest view of myself. It does not disparage my worth as a human being made in the image of God, but neither does it think everything should follow my will.

Thus, humility enables me to examine the cause of my anger more honestly. With humility, I am more truthful in answering the following kinds of questions: "Is there really an injustice here? Do I have a right to get mad over the matter? Or am I wrong to expect something to be the way I want it to be? Am I being self-centered? Or am I in a bad mood, so that I'm prone to get angry about things I should not be angry about?"

As long as we are on this side of heaven, we will suffer to some extent or on some occasions from self-centeredness. That means that we will probably succumb now and again to the unrighteous anger of the self-centered. But the more we advance in humility, the less often this will be. And even when we succumb to unrighteous anger, humility, along with patience, will enable us to see that the anger is unfounded.

Charity and Detachment

To close, I want to look at one more virtue that helps us to avoid the bad effects of anger. It is the greatest virtue of them all: charity.

In one sense, it is obvious that charity helps against anger. We can see that having charity toward our neighbor will work against our being too harsh to our neighbor out of anger. But there is a deeper way in which charity works against the vice of anger. To see it, recall that charity is a theological virtue. That means, among other things, that it is directed primarily to God. Charity is ordered to God even more than toward our neighbor. Of course, loving God and loving neighbor are inseparable. But loving God — that is, having charity for God — is first.

Yet it is awkward in contemporary English to speak of showing charity to God. We easily speak of showing charity to our neighbor, but to show charity to God? We want to reply by saying: "God does not need our charity!" To get around this awkwardness, we sometimes drop the word *charity* and use the word *love* instead. This is fine, but there is something worth noting about the word *charity*.

The word *charity* comes from the Latin word *caritas*. And *caritas* is derived from *carus*, which means "dear," as in "to hold something dear." The same Latin words, in fact, are at the root of the English word *cherish*. And indeed, to show charity to God is to cherish Him. It is to hold God dear, to value His presence in our lives. And we will do this all the more strongly if we not only cherish God with our wills but also deeply like Him with the emotion of liking, as described in chapter 2.

Now, if we hold God dear and cherish Him, this helps against the vice of anger. How? Well, when we do not cherish God, we cherish other things in place of Him. Of course, it is OK to cherish other things, especially other people. But it is not OK to cherish them in place of God, for then we cherish them wrongly. We hold them too tightly. We become attached. On the other hand, when we cherish God most of all, our grip on other things and people becomes less tight. And not holding on to other things so tightly, we become detached.

Being detached in this way is a great help against anger because when we hold something too tightly, we get angry when anything threatens or disturbs it. If am attached to how egg salad is made, I get angry when it is made in a different way. Or if I am attached to another person, I am easily miffed when that person does not do as I prefer. On the other hand, if I am detached, I am not so easily bothered.

So, to lessen the influence of anger over us, sometimes we need to let go. We need to become more detached. Some things are worth insisting upon and even fighting for, but not everything. There are things that we need to become less attached to. And again, the way to become detached is to cherish God more than anything else. We want to become attached to God rather than to creatures.

When I cling to God by cherishing Him first and foremost, I loosen my grip on other things. In turn, I am less disturbed, less likely to be provoked to anger when things do not happen as I like. Even if things do not go as I like, the one whom I cherish and hold dear above all — namely, God — is still there. He does not go away. He is my peace and solace. As St. Teresa of Ávila says, "Whoever has God lacks nothing; God alone suffices."

Conclusion

I have not spoken about the good purpose of anger except for a few comments. So, before ending this chapter, I would like to give a summary of how anger can be good. Anger can serve a good purpose by being a protest against a genuine injustice, such as a sinful tendency in ourselves or a wrong in the world around us. With this protest, we are not content with the injustice, and when possible, we work to correct it. But for anger to be good, there must be a real injustice behind it, not a fictitious one. Also, the urgings of anger must not control us; instead, we must have control over them, so as to direct the energy of anger in constructive ways. As noted, the virtues of patience, humility, and charity are especially important here.

All the saints had these three virtues, but I am especially reminded of St. Thérèse of Lisieux. The Little Way that she taught cultivates charity, humility, and patience. And it is worth noting that her Little Way is especially based on trusting in God's love. So, as Saint Thérèse grew in these virtues particularly by trusting in God's love, may we do the same.

....

Glory be to the Father and to the Son and to the Holy Spirit;
as it was in the beginning, is now, and ever shall be, world
without end. Amen.

CHAPTER 5
Good Grief

.... **PRAYER** ....

Lord, You do not want us to lose hope in Your power to
save when we face trials or are discouraged by our sin-
fulness. Therefore, have pity on us and renew our listless
spirits by being with us on the journey. Through Christ
our Lord. Amen.

Imagine that you live in an apartment and the person next
door is playing a kind of music that you dislike. But you hear
it only faintly, so you feel no need to do anything about the situation. Yet, a little later, your neighbor turns up the music. Now it
is so loud that you are moved to do something about it, whether
that means putting in earplugs or asking your neighbor to turn
down the music.

This is what the emotion of sorrow does. It amplifies, or
turns up, the volume on our disliking for something. We already
found the thing disagreeable and thus disliked it. But at first,
the thing was at a distance, and so we easily ignored it. Now the
thing is not at a distance but is upon us. Now our disliking be-

comes stronger. Our disliking for the thing deepens so that we are moved to do something. I offer this as a preliminary sketch of how sorrow is helpful. Much more needs to be said, of course, but we can initially say this: Sorrow is helpful because it deepens our disliking for some disagreeable thing that has come upon us, so that we are led to deal with the matter. In this way, sorrow is good.

Sorrow is one of those emotions whose good purpose can be hard to see. It is like fear and anger in this way. To be sure, sorrow has its bad forms which are to be avoided. But the same is true of every emotion. Even emotions such as hope and love (or liking), whose good forms are easier to see, also have bad and unhealthy forms. So with sorrow, as with the other emotions, we have to discern when it is good and healthy and when it is not.

Now, when I say that sorrow can be helpful, I am not simply saying that it is understandable to feel sad. Sometimes people reassure a person who is sad by saying, "It is OK to be sad." This can be a valuable thing to say. It assures the person that it is un-derstandable to experience sorrow and is a reminder that one should not feel bad about experiencing this emotion.

But I could also tell a sick person to be patient with recovery. Thus, if a friend catches the flu and is upset at having to stay in bed because she has so much to do, I might reassure my friend by saying, "It is OK to get sick now and again. It happens to us all. It's not your fault." This is true. But even so, I am not telling my friend that her sickness is itself good and helpful. So, while it is true that it is all right to experience sorrow sometimes, I am say-ing more than that here. I am saying that the emotion of sorrow can be good and helpful.

Some pre-Christian thinkers in the ancient Greco-Roman world did view the emotions as sicknesses. They were consid-ered sicknesses of the soul, and the goal was to be free of them. To be fair, often these thinkers had in mind the *bad* forms of the emotions when they called them sicknesses. In turn, some of these ancient thinkers spoke about alternative forms of the emotions that were good. But even when they spoke of good forms of the emotions, they did not include sorrow as one of the emotions that could have a good form. To their way of thinking, it was OK to be sad now and again, just as it was understandable to get sick now and again, but the sorrow itself was not good, just as a sickness was not good.

Saint Augustine explicitly rejects this view and instead argues that sorrow can be good. In his *City of God*, he even notes that there is something wrong with a person who is never sad. After all, there are evils in this world to be sorrowful about, and insensitivity to these evils is a defect. In the same vein, St. Thomas Aquinas writes in his *Summa Theologiae* that "it is a condition of goodness [in a person] that, should there be an evil present, sorrow or pain should ensue."

We sense the truth of this when we criticize people for being unmoved by tragic events. For example, I heard of a real estate investor who was making business calls in the New York metropolitan area on the day of the September 11 terrorist attacks. Unmoved by the disaster, he kept up business as usual. We rightly sense a defect in this man's character.

When bad things happen, we should have sorrow. Notice, though, that the bad things that cause sorrow are different from the sorrow itself. In the introduction, I noted that an emotion is a felt reaction. This means that sorrow is a response to something. In particular, it is a response to something bad happening. The bad thing that happens is one thing, and the response to it is another. The bad thing is, of course, bad, but the response can be good.

Sorrow responds to some bad, disagreeable thing by deepening one's disliking for the thing. And this response can be helpful, since it leads a person to do something about the matter.

What Is Meant by *Sorrow*

I am using the word *sorrow* here as a generic term to cover many versions of the emotion. Just as fear can have different versions, such as worry, alarm, fright, and dread, so sorrow has different versions, such as suffering, grief, pain, disappointment, mourning, sadness, and discomfort — to name only some. In the introduction, I compared this variation of an emotion to the variation of the color green. There are many versions of green, such as dark green, vibrant green, olive green, and so on. Still, we can refer to them all by one general term, *green*. Just so, I am referring to the many versions of this emotion by the general term *sorrow*.

As a general term, *sorrow* is not perfect. It tends to bring to mind a certain kind of suffering, that is, an interior suffering of the soul. Thus, it is sometimes distinguished from pain, which is then taken to be a suffering of the body rather than of the soul. The general term *sorrow*, however, covers both physical pain and interior suffering. Perhaps the word *discomfort* would be a better general term, since all versions of this emotion entail a lack of comfort. But the problem with the word *discomfort* is that it tends to signify something mild, whereas some versions of sorrow are frightfully intense, such as excruciating pain.

The word *suffering* could work as a general term, since all versions entail suffering something bad or disagreeable, as I will explain further in a moment. Yet this word, too, has connotations that do not fit all the versions. So, not having a clear alternative, I will continue to use the customary word *sorrow* to cover the different versions. But I will occasionally mix in other words, such as *grief*, *pain*, and *suffering*, to remind us that there are many versions of this emotion.

Whatever the version, each instance of sorrow arises from the same perception: that something we dislike has happened. This is the perception that leads to sorrow: We perceive that something we find disagreeable and thus dislike has befallen us.

This makes sorrow the opposite of joy. As noted in chapter 2, we have joy when we attain what we like. So, in the case of joy, an agreeable thing has come upon us. Of course, this is what we want. And various emotions work toward this end, especially the emotions of liking and desire. But when a disagreeable thing comes upon us, that is not what we want. And various emotions work against this, especially the emotions of disliking and aversion.

We have already described the emotion of disliking. Again, we dislike something we perceive to be disagreeable. The emotion of aversion arises when we perceive that the thing we dislike may come upon us. It comes near, and there is the possibility that it will befall us. We then experience aversion toward it. We are, in a way, pushed away from the thing so as to avoid it. But if the disliked thing still befalls us, then we have the emotion of sorrow.

To give an example, I dislike the taste of liver. So, when my dinner host places a dish of chopped liver in front of me, I experience the emotion of aversion toward it. I feel a repulsion toward it. Then, when I eat the liver, since it would offend my host if I did not, I have the emotion of sorrow. The disliked, disagreeable thing — the taste of liver — has come upon me!

When I say that sorrow arises from something I dislike happening to me, this does not mean that I cannot be sad about the plight of others. That is, it does not rule out feeling compassion for others. I can see what is happening to others as though it were happening to me. I can identify with others and come to see their plight as my own. In this way, when I see others suffering something disagreeable, I feel sorrow about it.

This ability to identify with others can also work with joy. I can have joy over the good things others enjoy, even though I do not have those things myself. As Saint Paul indicates, we can rejoice with those who rejoice, and we can weep with those who weep (see Rom 12:15). Of course, we *should* do so at times. Part of caring about others is identifying with their situations, both good and bad.

Sorrow in the Bigger Picture

Step back for a moment to recall the big picture. We are on a journey to God. We believe that God is the most agreeable thing there is for us and that when we attain perfect union with God in heaven, we will have the fullness of life. But on the way to God in heaven, we seek after agreeable things on earth. When we find things to be agreeable, we sense that they will contribute to our fulfillment and thus bring us closer to the fullness of life. As I will explain further in chapter 8, these agreeable things lead us on to God when we seek them correctly.

On the other hand, we also encounter disagreeable things on the journey to fulfillment in God. When we perceive them to be disagreeable, we sense that they would frustrate our fulfillment, and so we try to avoid them. In chapter 2, we noted that avoiding the disagreeable things that we dislike is not an end in itself. We do it in order to seek the agreeable things we do like. We avoid the one to attain the other. In fact, if we do not avoid the thing we dislike, we cannot attain the alternative thing that we do like. Thus, if I do not first avoid eating liver, I cannot then enjoy a hamburger.

Here is where sorrow fits in. It indicates that we have not avoided the thing we dislike. After all, sorrow arises when the disliked thing has come upon us. And if we failed to avoid what we dislike, that means we have not gone on to attain what we do like. Sorrow, therefore, tells us that we have failed to get what we like. It signals a failure in our striving for fulfillment. It says that we did not attain something we perceive would contribute to our fulfillment.

This does not mean that we always perceive a failure when we experience sorrow. What we perceive when we experience sorrow is that something disagreeable has happened to us. Sometimes a failure to obtain what we want *is* the disagreeable thing that we perceive has happened to us, but not always. I can have sorrow by failing to obtain the hamburger I want, but I can also have sorrow from eating liver without any further thought of what I would alternatively like to eat.

Still, whenever we have sorrow, it tells us that we failed to get what we find agreeable. Both Saint Augustine and St. Thomas Aquinas make this point. It explains why there is a note of frustration in sorrow. The experience of sorrow is the experience of being held back, if not set back, in our pursuit of fulfillment. Once we reach God and find our fulfillment in Him, we will be completely happy and at rest. But before then, we are always striving after what we think will bring us closer to the fullness of life. When we experience sorrow, it tells us that something is holding or pushing us back in this pursuit.

Awareness of a Problem and Motivation to Be Rid of It

It is good to know when we are not making progress toward a goal or are even moving away from that goal. Not making progress toward a goal is like standing on an elevator for a couple of minutes before we realize that we never hit the button to tell the elevator which floor to go to. And moving away from a goal is like missing the exit off the highway, when we are on a long road trip. Driving on for a while in the wrong direction, we end up farther away from our destination. Again, it is good to know when such things are happening so that we can correct the situation and get back on track.

In fact, if GPS apps such as Google Maps had alerts to tell us when we miss an exit, that would be helpful. (Perhaps they do, and I do not know of it.) Even without that, the voice feature on the GPS app says that it is recalculating the route, which can alert us that we missed a turn. In any case, it is helpful to know when we are not going in the right direction, as this allows us to correct the mistake before we get very far off track.

This is what sorrow does. It alerts us that we are *not* moving toward a desired goal or that we are being led further away from a goal. It signals that we are being frustrated in our pursuit of the ultimate goal, which is human fulfillment.

I came across a helpful example for explaining this when thumbing through a reference book, the *Dictionary of Moral Theology*. Under the entry for "Suffering," the author notes that we see a doctor when we are experiencing pain. The pain, which is a version of sorrow, alerts us that something is wrong. We naturally strive for health, and the pain is a sign that we are, or may be, veering from the goal of health. So, the pain makes us aware of a problem and leads us to address it by going to a doctor. The doctor then helps us diagnose the problem so as to heal it.

This brings us back to the good purpose of sorrow. Just as sorrow is helpful by leading us to address a problem, so bodily pain, as an instance of sorrow, is helpful when it leads us to address a health problem by seeing a doctor. But now we can note two parts within this. The first part is to help us to see that there is a problem. If you have a health problem but never experience pain from it, you might not become aware of the problem in the first place. The health problem itself is not good, but the pain that alerts you to the problem is good. If there wasn't pain, the problem might have gone unnoticed and never been treated. So, the first part of how sorrow helps us is by making us aware that there is a problem.

Notice that I am here using the word *problem* as shorthand for the situation that causes the emotion of sorrow to arise. Again, the situation is that of some disagreeable thing coming upon us and frustrating our pursuit of an agreeable thing that would contribute to our fulfillment. Thus, when we speak of a health problem, we are referring to the situation in which a bodily ailment has come upon us and is frustrating our pursuit of bodily health. But, of course, there are problems other than health problems. We can have a problem with our computer or with a relationship. In each case, something we dislike has happened to us and is preventing us from attaining the alternative thing that we like.

When some disagreeable thing happens to us, sorrow deepens our disliking of it. Our disliking is amplified. It screams, "I do not like this thing!" And this grabs our attention, as if to say, "Look, there is a problem here that needs to be dealt with!" So, if we were not already aware of the problem, sorrow makes us aware of it.

The second part of how sorrow helps is by giving us the motivation or the energy to deal with the problem. Again, this follows from sorrow's amplifying or deepening our disliking for the disagreeable thing that has befallen us. When the disagreeable thing is no longer at a distance but is upon us, we feel our dislike for it more deeply. In turn, our aversion grows stronger. And so, we are more deeply motivated to be rid of it.

Sometimes we need this extra dose of motivation. We can already know of the problem and yet ignore it and thus do nothing. For example, a man might know that he has poor health due to bad eating habits, but he lacks the motivation to change his diet. But when his poor health eventually leads to aches and pains, that gives him the motivation to deal with his health problem. He didn't need the pain and discomfort to make him aware of the problem, for he already knew about it, but he needed them to motivate him to do something about it.

Other times, we do not need sorrow or pain to motivate us. For example, a woman might experience pain in her stomach and go to the doctor. Her doctor discovers that she has ulcers. Thus, pain made her aware of the problem. But she can be sufficiently motivated to treat the problem without enduring further pain. Therefore, she takes medication to eliminate the pain, and even when she no longer feels pain, she cooperates with the treatment to heal her stomach.

But again, sometimes we need sorrow to motivate us. This is especially so when we have become complacent with a problem. Consider a husband who is in the habit of spending Saturday nights with his friends. His wife wants him to be home with her on those nights. She explains that it is one of the few times the two of them can spend quality time together. But he counters that it is also one of the few times he can be with his buddies. He realizes that this is a problem in their relationship, but he would rather not deal with it, and so he doesn't.

But suppose the issue comes up again. His wife again tells him that she would like him to be home on Saturday nights. But he again makes excuses. After their exchange, she goes to another room and cries. She does not know it, but he overhears her crying. He feels bad. It pains him to hear his wife cry. So, he resolves to address the problem and to talk with his wife about it further so that they can work out a solution.

In this case, the husband already knew that there was a problem, but he needed motivation to deal with it. That motivation comes from the sorrow he feels for his wife. This is also a case of having sorrow due to another person's experience of something disagreeable. That is, the husband's sympathy for his wife makes what was disagreeable to her disagreeable to him as well. When we care about others, their problems become our own. Then we become motivated to do something about the problems they experience.

Here we can see how sorrow's motivation can be valuable for doing works of mercy. Many people suffer from hunger, violence, harmful ideas, and other afflictions. Of course, we cannot address all the bad things that happen to others. If we tried, we would wear ourselves out. Still, that does not mean we can do nothing. We should do something to help others, something that is within our ability.

Yet sometimes complacency gets in the way. In such cases, we do not care enough about others. The scope of our concern is too narrow. We see someone dealing with a difficulty, but we think, "That's not my problem," so we do nothing. Again, it is not as if we can make every problem out there our own problem to deal with. But if we think, "That's not my problem," too often, we resemble Cain, who said, "Am I my brother's keeper?" (Gn 4:9). We need the courage to keep our scope of concern sufficiently broad. Then we let some of the bad, disagreeable situations that come upon others also come upon us. Their sorrow is our sorrow; their problems become our problems. And this motivates us to do something to help them.

If we fail to have compassion in this way and instead do nothing for the suffering of others, then we risk hearing those dreadful words at the judgment: "Depart from me, you cursed, into the eternal fire … [for] as you did it not to one of the least of these, you did it not to me" (Mt 25:41–45). Thus, the motivation that comes from sorrow can help save our souls, and in this way, sorrow surely serves a good purpose.

The Deeper Problem and Its Cause

Once we are aware of a problem and are motivated to get rid of it, we can set to work to eliminate the problem. And yet sometimes the way we go about solving a problem only creates more problems! To avoid this, we need to diagnose the cause of the problem correctly. The example of going to the doctor shows this. Before the right treatment plan or cure is put in place, the real cause of the health problem must be diagnosed. Then we can work to eliminate the problem correctly. We can solve the problem at its cause. And the sorrow we feel deepens our disliking not only for the problem but also for its cause.

Let us apply this to the journey of conversion. The problem we face on the journey to God is our fallen condition. We seek union with God by knowing and loving Him, and when that union is perfect, we will be fully alive. But that is not our situation now. Instead, we are away from the Lord. We have been reconciled with God through Jesus Christ, and we are journeying to God, but still we walk in the shadow of death and a valley of tears (see Ps 23:4; Ps 84:6, LXX; and the Hail, Holy Queen). And it is not only that the situation around us is bad, but that we ourselves are not well. We still have sinful tendencies that darken our intellects, so we easily misunderstand God and His ways, and they tempt us to stray from God, even when we do know His ways. And if we also consider the burdens experienced by those who have not yet been reconciled to God through Christ, the problem becomes even more sorrowful.

We need to diagnose the cause of this problem. What is the cause of our fallen condition? It is sin. The world fell into its current condition when sin entered the world through the disobedience of Adam and Eve.

To be sure, not everyone agrees with this diagnosis. Others agree that the world is in a bad condition, but they diagnose the cause as ignorance, and in turn, they think that the more enlightened we become, the more we will solve all our problems. Still others diagnose the cause as a lack of autonomy and a lack of kindness. So, if people were free to do whatever they wanted and only refrained from hurting others and being unkind to others, then all would be well.

When people make these diagnoses, it directs their disliking toward what they identify as the cause. So, the first group especially dislikes ignorance and puts great emphasis on education as the solution. And the other group especially dislikes restrictions on autonomy as well as people who are deemed mean or offensive. Ironically, they even become hateful toward those they consider to be mean and offensive!

There are partial truths in these diagnoses, but the people who make them fail to see that the root cause is sin. Note that I am calling sin the *root* cause. The fallen condition of this world is the general problem that includes all the other problems we suffer — from sprained ankles to the loss of loved ones. When Adam and Eve sinned, they turned from God and took the human race out from under God's protecting care. This has, in turn, exposed us to all the bad, disagreeable things that befall us. So, whenever we or others suffer something disagreeable, we can trace this back to sin. Sin is the root cause of this fallen world and all its problems.

But this does not mean that sin is the *direct* or *immediate* cause of all our problems. It is the *root* cause, not the *immediate* cause. In other words, many of our problems are not directly due to sin. In the Gospel, before restoring sight to a man born blind, Jesus stated that the man did not suffer blindness due to a sin committed by him or his parents (see Jn 9:3, 34). This is important to acknowledge. There is a human tendency to think that whenever we suffer a hardship, it means that we did something wrong. Job's friends made this mistake about Job, but we need to avoid it — whether we are thinking about our own problems or those of others. Of course, some problems I experience are directly due to sins I have committed. For example, I may experience a problem in a friendship because I gave in to anger and said something I should not have said to my friend. But not every problem I suffer is due to a sin I have committed. We can be doing everything right and still suffer problems, as did Jesus.

When sin is not the direct cause of a problem, we shouldn't expect the avoidance of sin to make the problem go away. Of course, we should always avoid sin. But to fix a problem where sin is not a direct cause, we must identify what the direct causes are and address them. So, if the cause of the pain on the right side of my abdomen is appendicitis, that is what needs to be addressed.

Still, sin is the *root* cause of every problem and the sorrow it causes. So, whenever a problem arises and causes us sorrow, the deepening of our dislike may be directed to sin as the root cause. To be clear, we *first of all* direct the deepened disliking toward the immediate problem and its direct cause, such as appendicitis. That comes first, and thus our sorrow motivates us to solve that problem as much as possible. We do not neglect the immediate problem.

But in a secondary way, we can also deepen our dislike of our fallen condition and of sin as the root cause. We see the immediate problem as a consequence of this deeper problem, and so we can direct our deepened disliking to sin as the root cause.

Curing the Sickness of Sin

Every suffering can deepen our disliking of the fallen condition of this world and sin as its root cause. I will say more in a moment about *when* we should take our sorrow deeper in this way. But for now, let us try to understand this better by returning to the analogy of going to the doctor.

Our fallen condition may be compared to a health problem. In a way, we are sick due to sin. And just as the pain from a health problem leads us to the doctor, so the sorrows of this world lead us to God, the Divine Physician, for healing. Like a doctor, God diagnoses the problem for us and tells us that its cause is sin. Sin has turned the human race away from God, in whom is our true fulfillment. It keeps us from being healed and from being given the fullness of life in God.

With this diagnosis, what is the prescribed cure? It is conversion. Sin has turned us away from God, and the cure is to turn back to Him. Thus, the cure or treatment plan is conversion.

Now, with many physical cures, the elimination of the health problem does not happen right away. And so here too. After we undertake the cure of conversion, our fallen condition is not immediately healed. The healing is a gradual process, a journey. But the journey will lead to our complete healing in God and even to partial healing along the way.

So, we have gone to the Divine Doctor and have received a diagnosis of the cause and a treatment plan to follow. Now what remains is for us to be good patients who follow the plan. And here we run into difficulties. Just as not all patients are good patients for their human doctors, so we are not perfect patients for the Divine Physician.

There are a few ways in which patients fail to cooperate with their human doctors. They can disagree with their doctors' diagnoses. And if they do accept the diagnoses, they can fail to follow the treatment plans correctly. Sometimes they do this because they find the prescribed cures to be difficult. For example, suppose a woman with heart disease is given medicine to keep her well, but it causes uncomfortable side effects, so she skips the medication on occasion. Another way in which patients do not cooperate with their doctors is by not avoiding the causes of their problems. Thus, a man might know that smoking is causing his pulmonary problems, but he likes smoking too much to give it up.

We can be poor patients of God in each of these three ways. But to make things simpler, let us say that we agree with God's diagnosis that sin is the root cause of our problems and that the cure is conversion from sin to God. Even so, we can fail to cooperate with the prescribed cure in the two ways mentioned. Sometimes we find conversion difficult, since it requires us to give up things and to endure difficulties. So, like the woman who avoids her medicine, we avoid conversion. And sometimes we do not want to avoid sin. Like the man who does not want to give up smoking, we do not want to give up sinful pleasures. Instead, we are attached to them.

We are not perfect patients therefore, but sorrow can help. If we accept the diagnosis that sin is the root cause of our problems, then, when we suffer, our sorrow can deepen our disliking for sin. In turn, we are more greatly motivated to reject sin and be rid of it, and this makes us more cooperative with our healing.

I was helped to see this by the Catholic theologian Fr. Khaled Anatolios in his discussion of the fourteenth-century Orthodox saint Nicholas Cabasilas in Anatolios' book *Deification through the Cross.* Anatolios notes that suffering can make us repudiate sin. What I have just said is my description of how sorrow can do this. It deepens our dislike for sin so that we are more firmly motivated to reject sin and to be rid of it.

Notice that conversion needs to happen on two levels. There is the conversion of our behavior, in which we turn from sinful actions and toward right actions. But there is also the conversion of our hearts. Even apart from outward actions, we need our hearts to turn from sin and toward God. Our hearts bear the sickness of sin, after all. We see this in the fact that we are not wholehearted in our love for God because we are not wholehearted in our rejection of sin. The heart needs to be healed of this. It needs to be converted more thoroughly from attraction to sin and to love of God.

Sorrow for sin helps with both levels of conversion. When this sorrow leads me to repudiate sin more firmly, I am strengthened to avoid external actions that are sinful. But at the same time, when I more firmly repudiate sin from my heart, my heart is healed. My sorrow over sin heals my heart of its attachments to sin so that it more fully rejects sin.

Sometimes when we suffer from a disagreeable thing happening to us, there is not much we can do about it. Yet we do have the option of turning our deepened dislike toward sin as the cause of all miseries. By simply sitting with the sorrow and letting it strengthen our repudiation of sin as the root cause of all the bad things in this world, we are being healed in our hearts.

This healing sorrow is how I think about redemptive suffering. We are being strengthened in our repudiation of sin. We thus turn to God and present ourselves, and even the whole world, to Him for healing. In this way, our sorrow can bring about healing not only for ourselves but for the whole world. That is, in a mysterious way, God uses our sorrow to bring healing for both ourselves and the wider world. He does this through uniting our sorrows to the sorrows of Christ, as we will see in a moment.

Before turning to the most perfectly redemptive sufferings of Christ, I want to give a word of encouragement and a word of caution. The encouragement applies to those who are discouraged because, like Job, they suffer even though they have lived upright lives, and they do not understand why this is so. The reasons some suffer in this way is mysterious, but still it may help for them to know that their suffering in these cases is not in vain but can serve a good purpose by being redemptive in the way just described. Through union with Christ's suffering, their suffering can not only heal their own hearts but also bring healing to the world.

At the same time, a word of caution is due in case anyone foolishly tries to take on many sorrows in an attempt to bring about lots of healing. Rather, we must discern carefully whether we are called to sit with a sorrow in this healing, redemptive way. The primary thing is to let the sorrow lead us to address the immediate problem that is causing it. We should let it give us the motivation to resolve that problem. Often that is enough.

But sometimes when we have a sorrow, God calls us to deepen the sorrow by letting it also become a sorrow for sin. Seeing the problem we are suffering as a consequence of our fallen condition helps us deepen our disliking for sin as the root cause of that condition. Indeed, we deepen our disliking for sin as that which has brought so much harm upon the human race, leading not only to our own suffering but to everyone else's. So, we more resolutely want the world to be rid of sin.

To dislike sin in this way requires in our hearts a firm love for God and the human race. And yet, when we suffer, can we maintain this love in our hearts? Note that even a small sorrow, such as the frustration caused by having to wait in traffic, can drive love from our hearts and replace it with an unrighteous anger. So, we should not presume to have the strength of love needed to suffer in this way. But again, sometimes God does call us to sit with sorrow in this healing way. And for those tempted to discouragement because they cannot eliminate their suffering or because they do not understand why they are suffering when they have tried to be faithful to God, it may help to know that their suffering is not in vain but can bring healing to the world.

The Redemptive Suffering of Christ

I have just argued that sorrow can make us better patients who cooperate more fully with the prescribed cure of conversion. But still, we are imperfect patients. We shirk conversion when it is hard, and we are attached to sinful pleasures. At times, our failure to cooperate with God's healing plan leads us to cry out with Saint Paul, "Wretched man that I am! Who will deliver me from this body of death?" But keeping us from discouragement, Saint Paul immediately gives us the answer: "Thanks be to God through Jesus Christ our Lord!" (Rom 7:24, 25).

In Christ we find the healing we need, for He became for us the perfect patient. Although He was without sin, He took upon himself the wounds of sin, and He perfectly cooperated with His Father to be healed of those wounds. In turn, we find our healing in Him.

I want to end this chapter with a quick meditation on how Christ became the perfect patient for our sake. We will look at both how He became a *patient* (that is, one in need of healing) and how He was the *perfect* patient (that is, one who fully co-operated in His healing process). We will see that He used the suffering of the Cross to do both.

For Christ to become a patient in need of healing is itself a marvelous thing, since He was without sin. Unlike us, He never sinned, and He did not have sinful inclinations. And yet He suffered the wounds of sin so as to need healing from sin. This is because Christ took upon himself all the ill effects of sin — all of them except estrangement from God.

It is not simply that Christ had compassion on us due to the afflictions He saw us suffer from sin. Yes, He grieved when He saw our afflictions, but He also suffered those afflictions himself. He was falsely accused and condemned, abandoned by friends, scourged, mocked, and crucified — in a word, He suffered the way of the Cross. Thus, He was wounded by our sins and became a patient in need of healing from the effects of sin.

In turn, Jesus became the *perfect* patient. He fully cooperated in the healing that God offers. He presented His wounded humanity to the Father for healing by giving himself to the Father in perfect obedience on the Cross. His path to healing was the way of the Cross!

We do not fully cooperate in our healing because it is painful. The cure of conversion requires that we let go of sinful attachments and push through hardships. The way of healing was also painful for Christ, since it was the way of the Cross. He did not need conversion, but still He experienced the hardships of conversion when He walked the way of the Cross.

Jesus had no sinful inclinations, but He had natural inclinations. He was naturally drawn to things such as bodily life and the support of His own people. Yet, to present himself in perfect obedience to the Father for healing, He had to let go of these, and that was painful. And the torments He had to endure in order to present himself to the Father on the Cross were painful. Still, He pushed through them and did not turn back (see Is 50:4–9).

How was Christ able to be so resolute in walking the way of the Cross for the sake of healing? First of all, His love for the Father and for us was so great. Loving God and us so much, He resolutely rejected sin as what offends God and as what most profoundly harms us. But it was not only His love that made His repudiation of sin so strong; it was also His suffering. Jesus used the suffering He endured to deepen His dislike for sin in the emotional part of His soul. In this way, He made His repudiation of sin total, rejecting sin not only with His human mind and will but also with the emotional part of His soul. That is, by means of the Cross, Jesus got the feeling part of His soul involved in His repudiation of sin so as to make that repudiation total. His suffering thus made Him even more perfect for the work of healing us (see Heb 2:10).

And so, we find our healing in Him who, like us, was wounded by sin but, unlike us, perfectly cooperated in His healing. Therefore, through His wounds we have been healed (see Is 53:5). Note that our share in His healing is a share in His repudiation of sin, and to share in His repudiation, we also share in His sorrow.

There are two ways in which we share in the sorrows of Christ. In one way, our love for Jesus makes His sorrows our own. Just as we feel sorrow for those we care about, so we feel sorrow when we think about all that Jesus suffered for our sake, since we care about Him. His sorrows become our sorrows. In the other way, our sorrows start off as our own. We are suffering from this or that problem, but we take that sorrow and unite to Jesus' suffering, as He wants us to do. Then our sorrow becomes His, and thus even our sorrows become redemptive for the world. In both ways, we share in the suffering of Christ so as to share in the healing of His resurrection (see Rom 8:17; 1 Pt 4:13).

Conclusion

Earlier in this chapter, I said that a bad thing that befalls us is one thing and the response of sorrow is another. The first is surely bad, but the second can be good. Just so, sin is bad, and so is our fallen condition. But sorrow is good if it deepens our disliking for sin and our fallen condition. In that way, we are more greatly motivated to turn from sin and to God. And so, we are helped on our journey of conversion.

....

Glory be to the Father and to the Son and to the Holy Spirit; as it was in the beginning, is now, and ever shall be, world without end. Amen.

CHAPTER 6

The Anger-Sorrow-Sloth Progression

·························· **PRAYER** ························

Lord, fill our hearts with Your light and Your peace. Give
us the grace to observe times of quiet so that we may
gain spiritual insight into ourselves, into Scripture, and
into Your will in our lives. Through Christ our Lord.
Amen.

The Seven Deadly Sins remain fairly well known in our culture, even while other parts of the Christian Tradition have been forgotten. One reason is that they are referenced in popular movies. But before the Seven Deadly Sins became a part of the Christian Tradition, there was a list of eight vices, called the Eight Thoughts, that were taught by early monastic authors. Over time, this list of eight became the list of seven with which we are familiar.

Both lists consider the order of the vices significant. While advancing in conversion, one would typically move from overcoming the first vice listed to overcoming the second, and then to the third, and so on. There were exceptions, of course. For instance, although one may have worked one's way down the list, that person might have to go back and contend once again with an earlier vice that he or she had overcome (lust was especially one that might have to be revisited in this way). It was also said that one or two vices might always remain a struggle for someone, even after that person had subdued the others. Still, the order in which the vices were listed was the order along which one typically advanced in the spiritual life.

So, it is noteworthy that one of the early monastic authors switched the order slightly. St. John Cassian learned the list of Eight Thoughts from his teacher, Evagrius, but later in Cassian's life, when he was teaching these vices, he switched the order of two of them. In ordering the eight vices, Evagrius had put sorrow before anger, but Cassian put anger before sorrow.

I learned the practical importance of this some years ago, when I was going through a difficult time. The difficulties I was going through made me want to give up on a work I had undertaken. Yet, when I talked to a monk from another monastery, he pointed out Cassian's ordering of the eight vices. In particular, he pointed out that after anger comes sorrow, and after sorrow comes sloth, or *acedia*. That was what I was experiencing: I had encountered some bad behavior, about which I was angry; I then became sad over the bad situation caused by the bad behavior. And then I began to experience sloth; I wanted to give up rather than do the task set before me.

In this chapter, I want to speak about this progression from anger to sorrow to sloth. Cassian does not say that all cases of anger lead to sorrow and then to sloth. But he observes that this progression can happen. And perhaps, like me, you have experienced it.

I think there is a hint of this progression in the *Rule of Saint*

Benedict. It is in the passage I cited in chapter 4, on anger. Again, it reads:

> The fourth step of humility is when in this very obedience, experiencing hard and adverse situations, or even when any injuries are inflicted, [the monk] embraces patient suffering with a quiet spirit and, bearing up, he does not grow weary nor walk away, for as Scripture says, "Whoever should persevere to the end, that person will be saved" (Mt 10:22); and again, "Let your heart be strong and be sustained by the Lord" (Ps 27:14).

I noted in chapter 4 how adverse situations and injuries can cause anger. Also, note how Saint Benedict says a monk can "grow weary" and "walk away." This growing weary and walking away sound to me like sorrow and sloth. One way in which we can grow weary and walk away, after getting mad, is by brooding a bit and then storming off in a huff. "I'm done," we say. "I've had enough of this," we angrily explain. Being mad, brooding, and quitting — that's a form of what I call the "anger-sorrow-sloth progression."

Regarding the three vices of anger, sorrow, and sloth, the vice of sloth is probably the least well understood. Sloth, which is also called *acedia*, is indeed hard to understand, partly because authors describe it in different ways. So, I should clarify how I understand it here. First of all, it has to do with the actions or activities we should be doing in order to advance on the journey to God. These include spiritual activities, such as praying and attending Mass, and also other things, such as doing our work, practicing work-life balance, and being attentive to the people in our lives. As a sort of shorthand for referring to these things we should be doing, I will call them the *critical means* for fulfillment. They are *means* in the sense of being things we do in order to attain our end — namely, fulfillment in God. And by calling them the *critical* means, I am indicating that they are especially important for us to do in order to make progress toward God. We should do them, and it would be negligent not to.

The kinds of actions and activities that belong to the critical means for fulfillment will vary to some extent as the circumstances in our lives change. Thus, when a married couple become parents, this brings new things they should be doing as part of their journey to God. Or, when someone retires from a long career, that person's critical means will no longer include the work he or she used to do. Sometimes the change will be temporary, in order to deal with a passing situation. For example, when someone is going through a difficult time, the critical means might vary to include practicing greater patience and paying extra attention to self-care. Given that the critical means for fulfillment can vary, we need continually to discern what they are in our present circumstances. And it should go without saying that doing these means as well as discerning them requires the help of God's grace.

But when we give in to the vice of sloth, we neglect doing some of these critical means for fulfillment. We experience a lack of motivation to do them, and not pushing through this lethargy in order to do them, we commit the sin of sloth. So, the sin of sloth is neglecting to carry out the critical means for our fulfillment because we find them hard to carry out due to a lack of motivation. And if we recall from chapter 4 that a vice is an abiding disposition to do a certain kind of bad action, then we can say that the vice of sloth is the abiding disposition to neglect doing the critical means for fulfillment due to a lack of motivation.

Three Concrete Examples

I will say more below about the vice of sloth as well as the vices of anger and sorrow. But before I do so, it will help to have some concrete examples of the anger-sorrow-sloth progression. In each case, someone is pursuing a goal and the attainment of that goal is thwarted, so the person gets angry, becomes sad, and finally experiences sloth.

The first example is the biblical story of Naboth's vineyard in the First Book of Kings. Ahab, the king of Israel, offers to buy Naboth's vineyard or to give him another piece of land in exchange for it. Naboth refuses the offer because the vineyard is his ancestral heritage. In turn, Scripture says, "Ahab went into his house vexed and sullen because of what Naboth the Jezreelite had said to him; for he had said, 'I will not give you the inheritance of my fathers.' And he lay down on his bed, and turned away his face, and would eat no food" (1 Kgs 21:4). Here, Ahab has failed to attain his goal. He gets angry, for he thinks that he should have been given what he wanted. But in addition to anger, sorrow comes upon him, and, in turn, he does not want to do anything, not even to eat. I'm taking this lack of motivation even to eat as sloth.

Another example comes from a monk who wanted to be elected abbot of his community. (I have heard of the following thing happening in three monasteries.) A talented monk in a monastic community does a lot for his community. There is talk of his perhaps becoming the next abbot — that is, the next superior of the monastery. What is more, this monk *expects* to become the abbot and wants this in his heart.

When the next abbatial election comes, however, he is not elected by his fellow monks. Because he thinks he should have been elected abbot, he becomes angry. Not being elected is an injustice in his eyes — hence the anger. Eventually the monk decides that the monastic life is not for him, and he leaves the monastery. Notice the irony: He goes from thinking that he should be the abbot, who is the spiritual father of other monks, to thinking that he himself should not be a monk. This is a tragic case of the anger-sorrow-sloth progression. The critical means for this monk's fulfillment naturally include the different activities he should be doing as a monk, but due to sloth, he neglects them and even abandons the monastic way of life.

A third example can be taken from something that occasionally happens to a young adult who is in a serious dating relationship and is thinking about marriage. Let us say that a young adult named Lucia has fallen in love with a young man named Max. They have been dating for a while, and their relationship has become serious; they have even been talking about marriage. But one day Max breaks off the relationship, and naturally, Lucia is devastated. Anger and sorrow alternate within her. At one time, it is anger that predominates; at another, sorrow. When she is angry, it is directed at Max, for she thinks, "How could he do this? He and I were so good together. He should not have done this." The anger and sorrow then give way to a kind of sloth. Given her stressful situation, her critical means for fulfillment at this time will include things such as reaching out to friends and family for support and keeping up normal activities in order to maintain stability during this rocky time. She lacks the motivation to do such things after the breakup with Max, however, so she mostly stays in her apartment and does not engage others.

Obviously, someone in Lucia's situation deserves compassion. It is possible for an experience like hers to be traumatic in the clinical sense so that the person would benefit from the assistance of mental health professionals. Also, the lack of motivation that results from such an experience can be a case of depression for which psychological or psychiatric help would be beneficial. The points I made in the introduction about availing oneself of such help apply here.

Without gainsaying any of those points, I want to offer an analysis of Lucia's situation, as well as of the situations in the other two examples, that draws on the understanding of the emotions presented in this book. Again, in each example, the anger-sorrow-sloth progression sets in when someone is thwarted in attaining a goal that was deeply desired. The analysis I am offering here has helped me when things I deeply wanted could not be attained, and I think it can help others who experience the same.

The Emotions Entailed in These Vices

So far, I have been speaking about the vices of anger, sorrow, and sloth and not about emotions per se. Vices are distinct from emotions, even though they are related to them. So, we need to look at this relation to see how emotions play a part in these vices.

Again, it was said in chapter 4 that a vice is an abiding tendency or disposition to do a kind of act that frustrates one's genuine fulfillment. Such an act is a sin, for to do an act that frustrates one's genuine fulfillment is against God's will. This means we may also describe a vice as an abiding tendency to commit a certain kind of sin. Applying this to the vice of anger, we can say that this vice is the tendency to commit the sin of anger. But what does a sinful act of anger entail? It surely entails a bad form of the emotion of anger. Yet if one simply has a bad form of the emotion of anger and does not consent to it, but instead resists its bad urgings, that would not be a sinful act of anger. No, the will has to go along, to some extent, with the errant emotion of anger in order for there to be a sin. This means that the vice of anger is a disposition not only to have a bad form of the emotion of anger but also to consent with one's will to that bad anger.

What about the other two vices, those of sorrow and of sloth? Again, the vice in question disposes us to act in a sinful way by disposing us to have an errant emotion and to consent to that errant emotion's urgings. So, the vice of sorrow is a tendency to be sad in a sinful way by disposing us to have a bad form of the emotion of sorrow and to consent with our will to that bad form of sorrow. When we speak of the vice of sloth, the key emotion in play is, I think, despair. With the vice of sloth, we are disposed to have a bad form of the emotion of despair and to consent to its errant urgings.

I have already spoken sufficiently about anger in chapter 4, but I have to say more about sorrow and despair. The previous chapter spoke about the emotion of sorrow, but I did not speak much about how it can take on a bad form, since I was trying to show how sorrow can be good. So, I will say more about bad forms of the emotion of sorrow and then turn to the emotion of despair.

Recall that the emotion of sorrow arises when we perceive that something bad — that is, something disagreeable — has come upon us. So, one way in which the emotion of sorrow can be wrong is when this perception is wrong. We perceive that something disagreeable has come upon us, whereas, in fact, that is not the case. In the examples we are considering, the disagreeable thing that happens to a person is that he fails to attain a goal he desired. But if the failure to attain the goal is not, in fact, a bad, disagreeable thing, then the sorrow that follows is out of place. This happens when the goal is morally evil, for the failure to obtain a morally evil goal is, in fact, good. For example, if I fail to take revenge on someone, that failure is actually good, and so I should not be sad about it.

The examples we are considering, however, do not involve pursuing a morally evil goal. In each case, the goal is morally permissible. After all, it is not necessarily wrong to want more land, as King Ahab did. Nor is it wrong for a monk to want to be abbot, if this is not motivated by worldly ambition but by a sincere desire to serve God and one's monastic community. Likewise, it was not wrong for Lucia to want to marry Max, granted that she had the right motives.

But another way in which the emotion of sorrow can take a bad form is when it is out of proportion. This is what is going on in these examples. One mourns over the failure to obtain a goal too much. As I said in the previous chapter, the emotion of sorrow deepens our disliking for a disagreeable thing that has happened. But here the deepening of dislike is excessive because the sorrow reacts to the disagreeable thing as though it were a greater misfortune than it is. To put it more succinctly, the people in the examples are sadder than they should be.

King Ahab should not be as sad as he is, for even though he failed to acquire Naboth's land, he has a lot of property already, and he does not need more land for his sustenance. Likewise, the monk should not be so sad because he was not elected abbot; in fact, he should feel some relief that he was spared the burdens of being in charge. So, too, with Lucia; her sorrow is exaggerated. It is not that she should not be sad. Of course, she should be. But she is *too* sad. She mourns as if more was lost than actually was.

In these examples, then, we have a bad form of the emotion of sorrow. But to be sad in a sinful way is not only to have a bad form of the emotion of sorrow; we must also consent with our will to what the bad form of sorrow is suggesting. In these examples, the exaggerated sorrow is suggesting that more was lost in failing to attain a goal than truly was. The people in our examples sin by consenting to this false suggestion. In Lucia's case, for example, we can guess that her exaggerated sorrow was suggesting to her that she cannot be happy without Max or that, when she lost Max, she lost the only chance she had to be happily married. But whichever suggestion it was, it was not true, and so she should have rejected it with her will rather than consented to it.

It is not that we should not be sad after we fail to attain a deeply desired goal but that we should not consent to what the exaggerated emotion of sorrow suggests. Also, when a person experiences an exaggerated form of the emotion of sorrow, that person still deserves sympathy. Failing to acquire something that one deeply desires is painful, and it is understandable if this leads to an exaggerated sense of one's loss. It can take time to process the flood of emotions that come in the wake of this. But eventually, often with help from the support and counsel of loved ones, a person should come to a clearer state of mind, see that the sorrow is exaggerated, and, in turn, refuse to consent to its suggestion that more was lost than truly was. The people in our examples, however, did not do this.

Turning to the emotion of despair and how it factors into the vice of sloth, we should first recall from chapter 3 that despair is the opposite of the emotion of hope. Both emotions apply to the situation in which an obstacle stands in the way of what we want. We have hope when we think the obstacle can be overcome. But we have despair when we think it cannot be overcome so that we cannot attain the goal we desire.

Notice that these two emotions determine whether we have the motivation in the emotional part of our souls to pursue a goal. Hope leads to the emotional energy to pursue a goal despite the obstacles, while despair takes that energy away. Hope is like the helium in a balloon. Just as helium fills a balloon and lifts it up, so hope fills our soul and lifts our spirits up in the pursuit of a goal. This lifting of our spirits toward the goal gives us the encouragement and the resolve to pursue that goal. Despair, on the other hand, is what pops the balloon. It deflates our spirits so that we do not have the energy to pursue the goal. Or, to use another metaphor, hope is what puts wind in our sails as we try to reach a goal, while despair is what takes the wind out of our sails.

As we saw earlier, when we have the vice of sloth, we do not have the motivation to carry out the critical means for fulfillment. Our spirits are deflated when it comes to carrying them out. This means that we have the emotion of despair, and not of hope, with respect to the critical means for fulfillment.

To understand this better, notice that, here, hope and despair are not simply responding to whether a goal can be reached, but to whether it can be reached *through a particular set of means*. Here, the goal is fulfillment, and the means being proposed are what we have discerned with our minds to be the critical means for fulfillment. But even though our minds tell us that these are the things we should do in order to advance toward our genuine fulfillment in God, the emotional part of our souls is not buying it. Instead, it is experiencing the emotion of despair toward the prospect of attaining happiness by these means. And behind this despair is the perception that these critical means for fulfillment will not lead to fulfillment. This perception sees these means as futile attempts to advance toward fulfillment; if anything, employing these means would be a waste of time and energy and would only work against our happiness.

With this perception and the consequent emotion of despair, we lack the motivation in the emotional part of our souls to carry out the critical means for fulfillment. Our minds tell us that we should be doing these things, but we lack the emotional energy to do them. We even have a distaste toward doing them. Often this is experienced when we should pray or go to Mass. We know with our minds that we should do so, but emotionally we lack the energy to do so. This is also experienced by students who know they should do their homework but lack the emotional energy to do it.

Again, we do not commit the sin of sloth simply by having a bad form of the emotion of despair. We sin when we consent to its urging. This bad form of despair urges us not to carry out the critical means for fulfillment set before us. If we consent to this and neglect to carry out these means, or at least neglect one activity within them, we commit the sin of sloth. This is what happened in the three examples we have been considering. I pointed out earlier what the critical means for fulfillment included for each person and that each person did not carry them out.

How do we fight against the temptation to sloth? In chapter 2, I said that sometimes we do not like doing the right thing but still we need to push through and do it. We considered the example of how sometimes we do not like to pray, but we must use our willpower to pray nonetheless. The same applies here when the emotion of despair urges us not to bother doing some activity within the critical means for fulfillment.

But the ideal is to have the emotional part of the soul support the mind and the will. And this requires the presence of hope rather than despair toward the critical means for fulfillment. Our minds have discerned certain activities as the critical means for fulfillment, and in turn, we set our wills on doing them. Next, we must cultivate the emotion of hope, which will provide the motivation to do those things in support of our wills.

How do we cultivate hope to overcome despair? In these cases, the emotion of despair is based on the incorrect perception that carrying out the critical means for fulfillment is not going to lead to fulfillment. Therefore, we want to counter this false perception by cultivating a correct one, which will give rise to hope instead of despair.

The correct perception will see that, although these means can be difficult and challenging at times, still they are the true path to fulfillment in God. After all, Jesus never said that the path to the kingdom would be easy. Rather, He said that "the gate is narrow and the way is hard, that leads to life" (Mt 7:14). And accordingly, the Letter to the Hebrews says, "You have need of endurance, so that you may do the will of God and receive what is promised" (10:36). Indeed, it is worth reading Hebrews 12:1–12 on this matter. The passage reminds us that the saints before us, and, of course, Christ himself, had to endure many difficulties on the journey to our heavenly homeland. It also explains that Jesus persevered through the Cross for the sake of the joy that lay before Him (see Heb 12:2). So, although "we must go through many hardships to enter the kingdom of God" (Acts 14:22, NIV), we do so for the joy that lies before us.

If we worry that the trials we must face will be too difficult, then let us rest assured that "God is faithful, and he will not let you be tempted beyond your strength, but with the temptation will also provide the way of escape, that you may be able to endure it" (1 Cor 10:13). God knows our weaknesses, and He will remain with us to uphold us through our trials. And if we give in to temptation, He is forgiving and bids us to get up and try again. God is extremely patient and forgiving, but at the same time, we must be sincere in our efforts to do His will.

By reminding ourselves of these things, we can form a correct perception that gives rise to hope. The perception is that carrying out the critical means for fulfillment, although difficult at times, will indeed lead us to true joy. When this perception gives rise to the emotion of hope, we will have the emotional energy and the resolve to do the things that truly lead to our fulfillment in God.

A Sinking Attachment

There still remains something to explain — namely, how being thwarted in attaining a goal leads us into the progression from anger to sorrow to sloth. I have said that the failure to attain a goal is what leads us into this progression. But why? It is because we are attached to the goal we have failed to attain, and we refuse to let it go.

It may seem odd to say that we fail to let go of a goal that we never attained. But this is possible when we see a goal as essential for happiness. We do not think we can live a fulfilling life without attaining the goal; instead, we believe that if we cannot attain it, we will be forever dissatisfied in life. This leads us to be attached to the goal in the sense that we cannot let go of the idea that this goal is necessary for our happiness. And as long as we perceive the goal as essential for fulfillment, we find letting go of it to be, if not impossible, then nearly so. To let go would be tantamount to giving up on the prospect of living a satisfying life and to thinking that we are doomed to misery.

Notice that this is consistent with the exaggerated sorrow we discussed earlier. Such sorrow reacts to the failure to attain a goal as though the failure were a greater misfortune than it truly is. This exaggerated sense of loss is bound to happen when we think a goal is necessary for our happiness. In that case, not attaining the goal would surely be seen as a great misfortune.

So, if we perceive that there is no way to attain a goal that is seen to be necessary for happiness, then we will experience a profound despair and despondency. Here we not only think that the means we first employed cannot get us to the goal, but we do not see any other means for attaining the goal. When this happens, our attachment to the goal contributes to sloth. After all, if we feel despair toward attaining by any means the goal necessary for our happiness, this will include the critical means for fulfillment. In turn, these means, like any others, are not seen to be worth the effort. Hence, we lack motivation to carry out the critical means for fulfillment, and we are tempted to sloth.

The despair and despondency might not be total. They might be mitigated by viewing fulfillment or happiness along a spectrum and making it our aim to maximize happiness and minimize misery. Then, when we think that a goal is necessary for happiness, we are really seeing it as necessary for *optimal* happiness, but we still think that without the goal we can be happy and avoid misery to some degree. So, we would still have the aim of maximizing happiness and minimizing misery, and we could have some motivation to employ means that are understood to contribute to this aim. But even if this provided some motivation for accomplishing the critical means for fulfillment, it would not be a very strong motivation. Rather, the hope to maximize our happiness and minimize our misery would be mingled with some despair that we will never be fully happy, as our hearts desire.

Our Christian faith does not teach that we should be content with partial happiness. Instead, we are to hope for complete happiness in the life to come, and even though we will not attain full happiness in this life, we are to hope and work for it during this life. It is even a sin to despair with an act of our will of attaining this perfect fulfillment in God. We may feel the emotion of despair toward attaining complete happiness in God, but we must not consent with our will to its suggestion that such happiness is not possible. That would be to deny that the all-powerful God is willing and able to save us. Rather, He is surely willing and able, and we should put our hope in Him, as I explained in chapter 3.

As we set our hope on complete fulfillment in God in the life to come, we experience some degree of this fulfillment even in this present life. As Saint Paul says (see Rom 12:12), there is a joy in hope, and therefore, as long as we live and work in the hope for complete fulfillment in God in the next life, we partially share even now in that joyful fulfillment. But again, the hoped-for aim is complete fulfillment in God — nothing less than that. Moreover, when we have the emotion of hope for this fulfillment, our spirits are uplifted in the pursuit of it, and we experience the motivation to carry out the critical means for attaining it, even though those means are sometimes difficult. But if we aim for less than full happiness with God, our motivation is mitigated, and sloth becomes a greater temptation.

So, if we refuse to let go of a goal in the sense that we hold on to it as necessary for happiness, then we will necessarily have the emotion of despair when we see that it cannot be attained.

By sapping us of motivation to do other things, that despair will lead to despondency. The more unhappy we think we will be without the goal, the greater the despair and the despondency will be. Indeed, we can enter a very dark place if we think that we will be miserable without attaining a goal and we see that the goal can no longer be attained.

This emotion of despair is excessive in that it excessively deflates our spirits. It should deflate our spirits toward the particular goal we are pursuing, since that goal cannot be attained. But it deflates our spirits too much: it also deflates them toward the greater goal of fulfillment, since it thinks that that greater goal is unattainable without the particular goal. Yet even with this flaw, this despair can serve a good purpose. When the emotion of despair takes the wind out of our sails and makes us despondent toward the goal we had been pursuing, that causes us to pause, and this pause is an opportunity to reassess our situation and make an adjustment.

Something similar happens in the biblical story of Balaam and his donkey (see Nm 22:21–35). Balaam sets out on a journey, but the donkey he is riding refuses to carry him to his destination. Balaam prods and even beats the donkey, but the animal refuses to cooperate. God then causes the donkey to speak, leading Balaam to realize that the donkey's refusal to carry him is for his own good. Likewise, when the emotion of despair arises, the emotional part of our soul refuses to carry us further in the pursuit of a goal, and in this way, it gives us the opportunity to reassess and adjust. We should adjust by no longer pursuing the goal and by moving on to pursue another goal.

But the emotion of despair cannot make this decision for us. It simply causes us to pause so that we have the opportunity to reassess and adjust. When this opportunity is given to us, there are three options for how we respond. The first option is the right one: We give up on the goal we had been pursuing and move on to another goal. But to do this, we must stop seeing the original goal as necessary for our happiness. If we succeed at doing this, then we also see that the proper object of the emotion of despair is not our happiness, but the original goal we cannot attain. Directing that despair toward the original goal, our spirits are deflated with respect to that goal, and this makes it easier for us to leave that goal behind and move on to another goal.

The second option is not to change anything. We refuse to let go of the original goal as necessary for happiness, and we simply accept that we will not be happy, since we can no longer attain the goal. In this scenario, we accept living in a state of despair and despondency. This seems to be how Lucia has responded to her situation, since she has isolated herself in her apartment. It is also how King Ahab at first responds, since he takes to his bed and refuses to eat. We will see, however, that King Ahab eventually adopts the third kind of response.

In the third option for responding, we still refuse to let go of the goal. But after our spirits are initially deflated by despair, we rally them by denying that the goal is, in fact, unattainable. We thus look for another way of obtaining the goal. We are determined to find some means, even if, by employing the means, we will make things worse. This is what King Ahab and the monk who wanted to be the abbot do.

If we read on in his story, we see that King Ahab is led to see another means for attaining the land of his neighbor Naboth. He has tried to obtain Naboth's vineyard through a fair exchange but failed. Then his wife, Queen Jezebel, leads him to see that he can obtain the land illegally through the murder of Naboth. Ahab's willingness to comply with this murderous plan shows that he has not let go of the goal of attaining Naboth's land. Rather, because he sees the land as necessary for his happiness, he is tragically receptive to the idea of murdering Naboth.

The monk also responds to his inability to attain his goal

by seeing it as only a temporary setback and by then finding an alternative means. But since he cannot be the abbot, he modifies his goal. He wanted something from being elected abbot. Perhaps it was power or status. Whatever it was, when he was not elected abbot, he did not let go of the thing he wanted; instead, he keeps pursuing it, but since he can no longer attain it in the monastery, he seeks it outside the monastic life. In this way, he holds on to the goal of enjoying power, status, or whatever it is that he seeks, but he leaves the monastery to seek this goal elsewhere.

Therefore, if we remain attached to our goal after failing to obtain it, there are two possible outcomes for us: We either let ourselves become despondent, as did Lucia, or we employ problematic means for attaining the goal, as did King Ahab and the monk. Neither outcome was a happy one for the people in our three examples. For Lucia, the bad result was despondency that led to isolation; for King Ahab, it was to partake in murder; and for the monk, it was to quit the monastic life. When we find ourselves holding on to our goals and sliding down the anger-sorrow-sloth progression, it may not lead to such disastrous results. But still, it can be spiritually harmful to us, if not also causing harm to others.

This brings to my mind a scene in a movie. The scene takes place on a nineteenth-century ship of war. A young officer commits suicide by jumping off the ship with a cannonball in his arms. The weight of the cannonball pulls him down to his death. If he had just let go of the cannonball, he could have floated back to the surface and breathed in new life. But he held on to the cannonball, which dragged him further and further down into the depths of the sea.

This serves as a powerful illustration of what can happen to us spiritually when we do not let go of a goal we can no longer attain. We can sink to a spiritual death through the anger-sorrow-sloth progression. To avoid this, we must let go of what we wanted. And as I have been saying, that requires no longer seeing the goal as necessary for a fulfilling life. Letting go is often very hard to do, but it is utterly necessary. We must let go and trust in God. We can find peace and happiness without the goal. We must let go of the cannonball so that we can resurface and breathe in new life!

In other words, we need to choose the first option given above: to let go of the original goal and turn to a new goal. Maybe the original goal was worthwhile when we first decided to pursue it, and maybe, if circumstances were otherwise, we could have attained that goal. But for whatever reason, we cannot attain it, and we need to let go and move on.

When we do so, we move on to another goal — or rather, to other goals. When we held on to the original goal, too much of our emotional energy was being drained by it. Now that this emotional energy is freed up, we turn it toward other goals that we had been neglecting. These goals — which can range from taking up a musical instrument as a hobby to deepening a relationship with a loved one — will be things we see as contributing in small or big ways to the ultimate goal of fulfillment in God. Seen in that way, they tap into our fundamental drive for fulfillment and are taken up into our hope for fulfillment in God, so we are motivated to do them for the sake of attaining that fulfillment.

But there is a particular goal toward which we should turn most of all after we let go of the original goal we had been pursuing. It is the goal of carrying out the critical means for fulfillment. The other goals help us on the journey to God in one way or another, but as we saw earlier, these means are those things that are especially important for making progress on this journey, so much so that we should not neglect them. Therefore, when our emotional energy is freed up by letting go of the original goal, we should most of all direct that energy toward the critical means for fulfillment. We should discern what the critical means are in the present circumstances and apply ourselves to them, fueled by the hope that comes from knowing that these means are especially the way to fulfillment.

In sum, when we are sinking into the depths through the anger-sorrow-sloth progression, we need to let go of the original goal we had been seeking and renew our commitment to other goals, most of all to the goal of carrying out the critical means for fulfillment. By cultivating the perception that these means are especially what will bring us closer to God and having the hope and motivation that this perception brings, we will resume our journey to God with renewed energy and vigor.

Letting Go of Essential Goods

But there is a final scenario we need to consider: What if the original goal we had been pursuing *is* necessary to our fulfillment? Thus far, we have considered cases in which the goal — attaining a piece of land, becoming the abbot, or marrying someone — is not essential for fulfillment. What about when a person wants something that is essential, such as bodily health, and yet the person cannot attain it? We can think of other things that are essential for fulfillment, such as loving relationships with others. What if these essential goods cannot be obtained?

In such cases, the anger-sorrow-sloth progression is still possible. Experiencing anger in this progression will be understandable and may even be appropriate. Also, sorrow will be inevitable if one loses an essential good. For example, if I lose good health, I will naturally mourn this. Of course, we should avoid sinful ways of being angry and sorrowful, but there may be good forms of anger and sorrow in these cases. Even so, we must avoid sloth. There is no good form of sloth. And as with the previous cases, the key to avoiding sloth here, too, is to let go of the original goal and renew our hope for fulfillment by carrying out the critical means for fulfillment.

But given that the original goal is something essential for fulfillment, there is a twist. As I said earlier, we should never give up on the goal of finding our fulfillment in God. Our God is a God of encouragement, and there is always hope in Him (see 2 Cor 1:3–7; Rom 15:4–5). So, when the original goal is something essential for our fulfillment, such as bodily health, we do not let go of this goal forever, but only for a time. We may have to let go of attaining it for a long period of time or even for the rest of our earthly lives, but we will not let go of it as a goal in the next life. We ultimately hope to have it in heaven as part of our fulfillment in God.

To understand this better, we will consider three examples of needing to let go of something that is essential for fulfillment. The essential things are bodily health, right treatment from others, and the avoidance of sin. And in addition to discussing how to let go of these, we will discern some of the activities that belong to the critical means for fulfillment in these cases. Doing these things will be the new goal that revives our hope for advancing toward the kingdom.

First Example: Loss of Good Health

First, consider the loss of one's health. We know that death awaits us all, and before we get there, some of us will lose elements of good health. It might be losing the ability to drive or the ability to walk; it can be losing our hearing or eyesight or some other aspect of good health. We have seen this in our families and in our communities. For those experiencing such things, it is worth knowing that your courageous dealing with the illness or limitation is a valuable witness. I have heard monks comment on how they admire a fellow monk for dealing so well with an illness or limitation.

We have in Scripture the story of the Maccabean martyrs. Not long before the coming of Christ, a mother and her seven sons all go to their deaths because they will not abandon the law of Moses. When the third son is presented for cruel torture and death, he stretches out his hands and says to the judge: "I got these from Heaven, and because of his laws I disdain them, and from him I hope to get them back again" (2 Mc 7:11). Notice that last line: "From him I *hope* to get them back again." When it comes to our health, we rightly hope in God to receive full health again in the next life. This will be part of our salvation in Christ.

Still, we may lose some element of health without the possibility of regaining it here on earth. We might have tried to recover it. Perhaps we even fought courageously to do so, seeing different doctors and trying multiple treatments. But we come to see that the recovery of our health will not happen. In such cases, we must let go. To do so, there will be a healthy despair, and we should use it to help us let go. This will be sorrowful and difficult to do, but it is the right thing to do.

In these difficult circumstances, what will the critical means for fulfillment be? They will include bearing the illness patiently or, if death is imminent, preparing for death by receiving the sacraments, expressing one's love for family and friends, and making any needed amends. By these means, we continue on the journey to God, and we have hope when we apply ourselves to them, for we see that we are thereby making progress on our way to fulfillment in God.

This is not Stoic resignation. The Stoics in the ancient world refused to set their hopes on anything that they could not ensure. Since they could not ensure bodily health in this life, they did not hope for it. They resigned themselves to not having good health forever. But Saint Augustine rightly rejects this in his work *On the Trinity*. In book 13 of that work, he rightly notes that, deep down inside, we cannot help but want full life and health for our bodies — and to want our bodies to enjoy such life and health for eternity. This leads Saint Augustine into a beautiful meditation on faith and on the Incarnation and Passion of Christ. Our faith is that God has the power, and has promised, to give blessed immortality to our bodies — not just to our souls but also to our bodies. God will do this if we walk in His just ways. One way in which God has showed us this is by raising up His Son after He suffered greatly and lost His bodily life.

To walk in God's ways while suffering an illness is not easy. We may be angry, especially toward God, since we do not understand why He allows us to suffer. And even if we are not angry, we will have sorrow over the loss of our health or some element of it. But we do not succumb to sloth, for, rather than despair, we hope to regain our health in the future and forever as part of our fulfillment in God, and in that hope we apply ourselves to the critical means for attaining this everlasting fulfillment.

Second Example: Loss of Right Treatment

Another example of losing an essential good is the loss of right behavior from others. Being in loving relationships with others is a necessary part of human happiness, and such relationships will entail that others treat us with respect, fairness, and honesty. But receiving respect, fairness, and honesty from the people around us does not always happen. When I mentioned earlier my experience of the anger-sorrow-sloth progression, it had to do with this. I encountered dishonesty and manipulation, and even a little bit of a smear campaign. Unfortunately, these things happen.

Such things can make a person resentful (which is a form of anger) as well as sad, and in turn, the person wants to give up. This is what I experienced. We want civil, honest behavior. Not getting it, we can start slipping down the anger-sorrow-sloth descent. To avoid this, we need to accept not getting the proper behavior that was expected. We have to let go of expecting it. And doing so can be very hard.

Indeed, something within us objects to letting go of this goal. We think: "If I let go of expecting these people to treat me rightly, am I then saying that it was all right for them to behave as they did? Am I then condoning their wrong behavior?" The answer is no — but it can feel that way.

This is hard not only to do but also to explain. In one sense, we still want others to act rightly. We don't let go of that. After all, if they would act rightly, that would be good for them, and love requires that we want what is good for them. But in another sense, we need to stop wanting them to act correctly. Or we might put it this way: We still want them to act rightly, but we have to stop expecting it. We can still want it, but we have to let go of expecting it.

This has been my experience in dealing with bad behavior from others. If I go on expecting them to treat me correctly even though they have shown that they are not going to do so, then I end up being continually upset. I keep becoming angry, nursing a grudge, and this can lead me to discouragement and sloth. At a certain point, the healthy thing is to let go. Let go of the expectation. Want the right behavior, but do not expect it.

Once again, this is not Stoic resignation. What keeps us from the quiet despair of Stoic resignation is our faith that God is just. Therefore, we hope that God will bring about perfect justice, if not in this life, then in the next. So, we will eventually be treated rightly, and in heaven, that right treatment will never end. We do not, then, despair of our fulfillment, which includes being treated correctly.

But what are the critical means for fulfillment in this situation? They include what is suggested by the Lord in the Beatitudes. He says that those who suffer for the sake of justice will have a great reward in heaven (see Mt 5:10–11). That is our new goal: to suffer for the sake of justice. In other words, it is to suffer as Christ himself suffered unjust treatment.

Notice what this includes. Suffering for the sake of justice as Christ did means patiently enduring mistreatment from others. Even though we are being wrongly treated, we do not react harshly or unjustly ourselves. We keep focused on doing what is right and good in God's sight. As Scripture says of Christ, "When he was reviled, he did not revile in return; when he suffered, he did not threaten; but he trusted to him who judges justly" (1 Pt 2:23).

Also, we must forgive those who mistreat us. Of course, this is very hard to do, but we know how insistent and demanding Jesus is about forgiving others. And it is for our own good that we forgive others, for if we do not, we are unlikely to let go in the way that I am describing. Rather, we will continue to hold on, as the man in the movie held on to the cannonball and sank into the depths.

Further, suffering for the sake of justice, as Christ did, includes charity toward our persecutors. As already noted, love requires us to want our persecutors to stop their bad behavior, since that would be good for them. Their amendment is not guaranteed, but we sincerely want, hope, and pray for it. We even endure our suffering with the hope that it might somehow contribute to their conversion as well as to our own conversion and that of the world.

So, if we no longer receive right behavior from others, we may need to let go of expecting it. This is not the first thing to do. First, as much as possible, we try to get the others to correct their behavior. But sometimes that does not succeed, and eventually we must stop expecting them to change. We must let go. But even as we let go, we hope for the justice that God will bring about eventually and in which we will find perfect joy. And to contribute to the coming of that day, we apply ourselves to the critical means for fulfillment, which, in this situation, especially include suffering as Christ did for the sake of justice. Doing so will lead to a great reward in heaven (Mt 5:12).

Third Example: Loss of Being Without Sin

As a final example, consider another loss of an essential good: the avoidance of sin. Surely, this is correctly desired as essential for true human fulfillment. But when we sin, we lose this essential good. And the anger-sorrow-sloth progression can also result from this loss.

Here is what the progression looks like in this case. We are journeying to the kingdom, striving for conversion so as to live a holy life. But along the way, we sometimes fail and sin. It may be that we give in to anger, lust, vainglory, or some other sinful behavior. We get angry with ourselves for having sinned, and then there is sorrow over the fact that we sinned.

In turn, we are tempted to discouragement. We might think, "I can't believe that I did that. I had been doing so well, and then I did this stupid thing! What hope is there? I am simply unable to avoid sinning." Or, if the sin is a habitual one that we have been struggling with for a while, we might be discouraged with thoughts such as, "There is no hope. I cannot avoid this sin. I have tried and tried, and I just can't do it."

As a sinner, I have experienced these discouraging thoughts myself. And as a priest, I have heard people say they are discouraged in this way and are tempted to give up the fight against sin, or at least to give up fighting against a particular sin. In some cases, they do give up. For instance, they think, "What's the use? I'm damaged goods," and then they no longer fight against a habitual sin. This discouragement is an unhealthy despair that results in a deadly sloth. We need to resist the descent into it.

To avoid this descent, we must once again let go of the goal that is acting like a cannonball pulling us into the depths. But the goal is not simply that of being without sin. After all, we are never to let go of that goal! Rather, we must let go of the goal of being without sin *by our own strength*. Due to the pride that lingers in us, we find ourselves clinging to the false idea that we can avoid sin *on our own*.

And yet this goal proves hard to let go of. Often without realizing it, we hold on to a sense of self-sufficiency. How, then, do we let go of this goal?

First, we should direct our despair after falling into sin. We should not let the emotion of despair lead us to give up trying to be without sin, but we should direct it toward helping us to give up trying to be without sin by our own power. Our repeated failure to avoid sin is showing us that we cannot do it by ourselves but that we need God's help.

So, let go of trying to do it on your own and apart from God. Instead, aim at becoming more and more united to God, at going deeper in your relationship with Him, and at letting Him live more deeply in you. In this way, you come to share in His strength, and by that strength, you can avoid sin. After all, "he who is in you is greater than he who is in the world" (1 Jn 4:4).

This, then, is an important part of the critical means for fulfillment to which we should turn in this situation. We are to go deeper in our relationship with God and to strive to do so through Jesus Christ. Through faith in His humanity and by living in Him through good works, we enter more deeply into His divine life, and that divine life enters more deeply into us.

This surely contributes to our fulfillment in God. After all, we are becoming more closely united to Him in whom is our fulfillment. God is the one who is most agreeable to us. So, not only does our closer union with God help us to avoid sin; it also brings us profound joy.

Being free of sin is surely essential for human fulfillment. And we hope for the day when sin will be no more. While we await that day, here on earth we sometimes fail to avoid sin. The despair we then feel tempts us to give up on the fight against sin. Instead, we should let the despair we feel help us give up trying to avoid sin by our own strength. And then let us work at going deeper in our relationship with God through Jesus Christ, for that will make us more able to avoid sin in this life, and it will lead us to the kingdom where sin will be no more.

Conclusion

Whatever is pulling us down, we need to let go of it. But we never let go of the hope of fulfillment in God through Jesus Christ, and until we attain that day, we apply ourselves in hope to doing the things that hasten its coming (see 2 Pt 3:12).

....

Glory be to the Father and to the Son and to the Holy Spirit; as it was in the beginning, is now, and ever shall be, world without end. Amen.

CHAPTER 7

Steps to Action

································· **PRAYER** ·························

Almighty God, we give You permission to change us so
as to conform us to Your Son. Or, if we hesitate to give
You this permission, we ask that You take away our
hesitations and make us trust and believe in You more.
Through Christ our Lord. Amen.

Plato gave an image of what it is like to govern the emotions. He said that it is like riding a chariot. The charioteer is the rational part of the soul — what I have been calling the thinking part of the mind. And the chariot has two horses that the charioteer needs to guide and control. The two horses represent the passionate part of the soul — that is, the emotional or feeling part. The reason there are two horses is that they represent the two parts into which the passionate part is sometimes divided, the concupiscible part and the irascible part. But as I said in the introduction, we need not worry about that subdivision.

Every metaphor has its limits. But there are a couple of reasons why I appreciate this metaphor. First, it shows that the emotions have a positive role. Just as horses play a positive role in pulling a chariot, so emotions contribute positively to our spiritual lives. Horses provide the energy to move the chariot where it needs to go. Likewise, the emotions provide energy. When rightly ordered, they give us the energy to advance in the journey that leads to God.

In these chapters, I have tried to show how the emotions, once converted, can work for our ongoing conversion in the Christian life. Just as a charioteer must harness the energy of the horses, so must we harness the energy of the emotions for our spiritual journey.

But to harness their energy, we need to reform them. As I have noted, this is very hard work at times. This provides the second reason why I like the metaphor of the chariot. Just as we need to train and discipline horses for them to be serviceable, so must we train and discipline the emotions.

I can't say that I know much about training horses. Still, I imagine that it takes some work. Like other animals, horses have their own instincts and impulses. They have "minds" of their own, so to speak. I've been told, in fact, that horses are very smart animals. Trainers must know how to work with them to bring them in line with the wishes of their human owners.

In a similar way, we must train our emotions. And this is probably harder than training horses. Who has completely mastered his emotions? Not me. But for all the hard work, the effort is worthwhile. When the feeling part works with the thinking part of the soul, we are integrated and can live more fully for the glory of God.

So, what I'd like to do in the remaining two chapters is offer some thoughts on how to train our emotions. In fact, the word *asceticism* comes from the Greek word for *training*. And when it comes to training our emotions, the first thing we need to do is to put a check on our wayward emotions. We need to stop acting on that disordered desire, unhealthy fear, or harmful anger. That's the topic for this chapter: putting a check on the urgings of errant emotions. In other words: How do we keep ourselves from following misguided emotions?

To be sure, saying no to wayward emotions is not the only part of training the emotions. We also need to get our emotions lined up with the right ways of acting — to persuade our emotions to move in the right directions. I will say more in the next chapter about persuading the emotions to go in the right directions. But first we need to consider how we can keep them from moving us in the wrong directions.

Origen and Steps to Action

To understand more fully what it means to say no to errant emotions, we turn to the early Christian writer Origen. He was not a monk and did not write for monks in particular, but he had great influence on monastic literature. The third book of his work *On First Things* presents an understanding of human thoughts that would influence Evagrius and others who speak of the Eight Thoughts. The thoughts, as Origen understood them, lead to emotions, which then prompt us to act in certain ways.

In this writing, Origen attempts to explain how human beings exercise free choice. Unlike nonrational animals, we do not have to go along with our urgings. We can say no to them and prevent them from becoming actions.

Origen says that behind the actions of animals are thoughts and emotions. Really, since animals lack reason, we shouldn't speak of them as having "thoughts" as humans do. It would be better to speak of them as having awareness or consciousness. They become conscious of something, and that leads to emotions, which then lead to action.

For example, take ducks. I used to raise ducks for eggs, and one thing I observed is that ducks have very good eyesight. They can spot a hawk flying very, very high above. When they become aware of a hawk flying above, this awareness leads to the emotion of fear. The ducks become still and keep quiet; they stop whatever they are doing. Now they are alert, keeping watch, often tilting their heads to keep a wary eye on the aerial predator. Their awareness of the hawk leads to the emotion of fear, which leads to the action of keeping watch. The steps are awareness, emotion, action.

The parallel in human beings is thought, emotion, action. We have a thought and then an emotion, and that emotion urges us to act in a certain way. Thought, emotion, action.

We should note here that the thought has a perception within it — the kind of perception that leads to an emotion. In other words, the thought is not simply a consciousness of something, but also an evaluation of it, a perception of whether the thing is good or bad and in what way. Because such a perception is within the thought, the thought leads to an emotion. Then the emotion urges us to do some action.

Now, with animals, the progression of awareness to emotion and then to action is inevitable. The duck sees the hawk and cannot help but have the emotion of fear and, in turn, carry out the action of keeping watch. But human beings are different. They can stop the progression that leads to action. And this is thanks to reason, says Origen. With reason, one can see whether the progression is a good or a bad one. If it is good, then one consents to it. But if it is seen as bad, one can withhold consent and the emotion does not translate into an action.

For example, suppose a man is exiting an airplane that has just landed. He is the last person getting off the plane, and as he walks by the empty seats, he sees on one of them a wallet, which someone apparently left behind. In fact, he can even see the edges of many green bills sticking out of the wallet. This wallet is stuffed with cash! The thought comes into his mind that he could simply take the wallet and slip it into his bag without anyone noticing. That thought, in turn, leads to the emotion of desiring the wallet for himself, and that emotion urges the action of taking the wallet. Again, the steps are thought, emotion, action.

But due to reason, this man can see that these steps are leading him in the wrong direction. Taking the wallet would be tantamount to stealing. Seeing with his reason that this is wrong, he can put the brakes on the progression of steps toward the action. Even if the desire to take the wallet persists, he can refuse to do the action that is being urged by this desire. In this way, says Origen, reason oversees the steps and can stop their progression toward action. That is why human beings, unlike nonrational animals, have free choice and are responsible for their actions.

Being able to stop the progression is a crucial part of reforming our emotions. This is because, if I give in to a wayward emotion, that emotion becomes stronger. But if I do not give in, the emotion becomes weaker. For example, the more I act out of an unhealthy fear, the more that fear controls me. Or the more I let myself be overcome by anger, the more anger consumes me. But if I can check the urgings of these emotions and not act on them, then their control over me diminishes.

After I had studied Origen's ideas about the progression from a thought to an action, I heard a talk by a priest who is also an addiction counselor. In particular, he counsels people with addictions to pornography — a very prevalent problem in our day. The priest pointed out that, when addiction counselors help people fight addiction, they sometimes counsel them to identify the steps that lead to the unwanted action.

The series of steps is called a *ritual*. I don't find this the happiest word choice, yet I believe that addiction counselors use the term because the series of steps *recurs* whenever the person is drawn to the addictive behavior. That is, like a ritual, the steps have a structure that is repeated.

So, note the parallel with Origen — an interesting parallel, I think. Origen identifies the steps leading to an action in order to show that we do not have to perform the action. Similarly, addiction counselors identify the steps leading to an action, the so-called ritual, in order to help people resist performing that action. Both indicate that seeing the steps that lead to an unwanted action helps us to avoid it. When we see how the movement toward the action develops, how it unfolds step by step, then we see opportunities to intervene and stop the development toward the action.

Now, someone might object to my drawing this parallel between Origen and addiction counselors. They would note that Origen was not talking about addiction in particular. And that's true, but there is still a parallel. Even though Origen was not talking about addictions, his teaching applies to habitual sins. The early monastic tradition thought so, and that is why they borrowed from his teaching to explain the Eight Thoughts, which are sinful ways that have, or at least can, become habitual. To be sure, a habitual sin is not necessarily a clinical addiction, but there are similarities. In both, one experiences an inability to break free from the unwanted behavior. And in both, there is a progression of steps leading to it.

So, if we find ourselves struggling against a habitual sin, it may be useful to step back and identify the steps leading to the sinful behavior. Now, while Origen gave the three steps of thought, emotion, and action, addiction counselors identify more steps than these. There are two additional steps in particular that I would like to speak about here. Although Origen does not mention these, there are hints of them in our Catholic tradition, as I will try to show. One of the additional steps comes at the beginning of the thought-emotion-action progression. The other comes between emotion and action.

Triggers

First, let's consider the additional step that is at the beginning of the progression. It is a trigger. That is, counselors speak of something that prompts, or triggers, the tempting thought and its consequent emotion. For example, the smell of tobacco may trigger the thought of having a smoke, which leads to the desire to smoke a cigarette and then to the action of smoking.

A lack of sleep can also work as a trigger. It can lead, for example, to overeating. The lack of sleep causes a sort of stress on our bodies, which can trigger thoughts of food as a means of alleviating the stress, and in turn, one overeats. Of course, the lack of sleep may also trigger other thoughts leading to bad behavior, such as being grouchy.

The acronym HALT can be helpful in identifying triggers. It stands for "hungry, angry, lonely, tired." These are common triggers for bad behaviors, and the acronym HALT was created to help us understand why we might be experiencing temptations to act wrongly. Being hungry, angry, lonely, or tired might be triggering the thoughts that lead to the emotions that are prompting bad actions.

It seems that these four things act as triggers by causing us stress. In each case, there is an unmet desire. With hunger, there is an unmet desire for food. With loneliness, there is an unmet desire for companionship. Being tired indicates an unmet desire for rest. Even anger involves an unmet desire — namely, an unmet desire for what is right and just. Now, when a desire is not satisfied, there is a sort of frustration in that, and therefore a kind of stress occurs. In fact, this stress is a form of sorrow, and as noted in chapter 5, sorrow motivates a person to do something to resolve the underlying issue. So, when we have stress, we are understandably prompted to find ways to alleviate that stress. And in searching for relief, tempting thoughts often arise — after all, not all the ways of alleviating stress are wholesome.

Not all cases of stress come from hunger, anger, loneliness, or tiredness. For example, there may be very difficult or painful things happening in our lives that naturally cause stress. Whatever the cause, stress makes us look for ways of alleviating it. And so, thoughts of things that can bring relief pop into our minds, and these thoughts can lead to disordered emotions, which lead to bad actions. The bad actions are attempts to find relief. I already gave the example of overeating as a way of seeking relief from stress. Other actions we might undertake to relieve the discomfort of stress include sexual sins, being rude (for don't we get a kind of relief from "putting a person in his or her place"?), and spending too much time on the internet or watching programs or movies (so-called binge-watching). Note that using the internet and watching programs or movies can be healthy ways of relieving stress. The bad action to which I am referring is spending too much time on these things.

Besides stress, another interesting example of a trigger is idleness. It's a fairly common trigger, in fact. A college student shared with me that during his Christmas break, he fell into bad behaviors, such as sleeping too much and spending too much time on his smartphone or computer. You see, while on break, he did not have classes, activities with friends, or other things to keep him busy in a constructive way. Rather, he would sit at home with nothing to do. He was idle. To escape the boredom of doing nothing, he would fall into the bad behaviors just mentioned. I have heard, too, that idleness is often a trigger for people struggling with addictions. In idle moments, thoughts of the addictive behavior can come to mind, and they can tempt the person back to that behavior.

Saint Benedict speaks about idleness in his teaching about the right arrangement of prayer and work in the monastery. In his *Rule*, he famously calls idleness an "enemy of the soul," and he gives instructions for monks who, during periods for reading, cannot read due to sickness or who will not read due to negligence. He says that they are to be given work to do so that they may not be idle.

Saint Benedict recognized that idleness creates a space in which bad thoughts can arise, and bad thoughts can lead to bad actions. In other words, idleness can be a sort of trigger for bad thoughts.

I don't know if Origen mentioned anything equivalent to a trigger in his writings. Yet there is a rough equivalent in the Catholic tradition — namely, occasions of sin. Occasions of sin are examples of triggers. I'm not comfortable saying that all triggers count as occasions of sin, but I do think that all occasions of sin count as triggers.

Here is why I am not sure that all triggers are occasions of sin: We tend to think of occasions of sin as preventable. We can avoid an occasion of sin, but we cannot always avoid triggers. As noted, stress is a trigger, and perhaps we can avoid it now and again, but can we always avoid stress? No. So, it is worth pointing out that not all triggers can be avoided.

But even if not all triggers are occasions of sin, it seems to me that all occasions of sin are triggers. And given that we should avoid occasions of sin, we see here that we should avoid certain triggers. In other words, although not all triggers can be avoided, some can.

Here is a lighthearted example: Sometimes at my monastery, we receive jigsaw puzzles as gifts. When we receive a puzzle, we put it in our community room, and eventually some monks will open the box and begin to work on the puzzle. Now, there is nothing inherently wrong with doing a jigsaw puzzle. What is wrong is when you spend hours each day on it. In my experience, that is a temptation, once you get going on a puzzle!

So, what is the occasion of sin or trigger in this case? It is when a monk is walking by the community room, and he decides to walk over to the puzzle to look at its progress. Going over to the puzzle is a fatal move! Once he starts looking at it, he is easily drawn in. So, the occasion of sin — in this case, the trigger for spending too much time on the puzzle — is putting oneself in the situation of being lured into doing this.

The Value of Identifying Triggers

Again, the point of identifying these steps is to be able to stop the progression toward the unwanted action. So, we can ask: "What is the value of identifying the trigger that sets off the progression toward the bad action? How can identifying the trigger help us here?"

For one, if we are aware of what triggers bad behavior in us, we can work to avoid it. If a lack of sleep is a trigger, then we need to work at the discipline of getting enough sleep. By avoiding the trigger, we are not letting the progression toward the bad behavior begin in the first place.

But as noted, not all triggers are avoidable. Stress can be a trigger, and we cannot always avoid stressful situations. Another thing that can be a trigger and yet cannot be completely avoided is the bad behavior of others. Someone might do something, such as using bad manners while eating, that triggers excessive anger, which pushes us toward bad actions, such as grumbling too much. Yet we cannot completely escape experiencing the bad behavior of others. Thus, Saint Benedict tells his monks to bear with the greatest patience not only the bodily infirmities of others but also their infirmities of behavior.

So, when you can't avoid encountering a trigger, is there still a value in identifying that trigger? I think so. There is a value in understanding what is happening within us when we are experiencing temptation. When we can name and thereby better understand what is triggering the progression toward bad behavior, we have more power over it and feel less helpless to resist it. We are able to think, "I see what is going on here, and I do not need to go along with it." It is not that the temptation completely goes away, but the power of the temptation is somewhat diminished.

Also, when we understand what triggers us, even when we cannot avoid a trigger, we are able to be on guard against its effect. That is, when we encounter the trigger, we can anticipate that it is going to set off a chain reaction, tempting us toward the bad behavior in question. Anticipating this, we can put ourselves in a better position to resist it.

There is another value to identifying the things that trigger us, apart from whether we can avoid them. Knowing our triggers can be an opportunity to reflect on whether we should be so "triggerable," so to speak. I cannot do away with all the triggers in my life, but maybe I can work at letting go of some triggers. Maybe I am allowing myself to be too easily triggered in some cases.

This is worth considering, especially when the trigger is what other people say or do. And that is often the trigger! What someone says or does can trigger anger, discouragement, or anxiety within us. But we should remember that we can't control what other people do. Yet, if we let them trigger us, or "push our buttons," then we are letting them control us. To illustrate this, I once drew a cartoon that showed a man covered with a lot of buttons. The point was that perhaps other people push our buttons often because we have too many buttons to push! Again, if we let other people trigger us so much, we are giving them a certain control over us. Don't let another person's behavior have a bad influence on you. Don't give the other person that much power over you.

Domineering Emotions

So much for triggers. We have now looked at these four steps: trigger, thought, emotion, action. The additional step mentioned by addiction counselors is in between emotion and action. Or we can say that it divides the step of emotion in two. There is the on-set of the emotion, and then there is an especially overwhelming experience of the emotion. With this overwhelming experience, the emotion dominates the psyche, as it were. It starts to take over. So, the progression becomes: trigger, thought, emotion, *domineering emotion*, and then action.

As for this additional step of domineering emotion, there is something of a parallel in our Catholic tradition. Let's exercise our minds a little by considering that first. This is a complex topic, and I am able to offer only a sketch here.

Within our Tradition, some have drawn the following dis-tinction. They note a difference between the first stirrings of an emotion and the subsequent urging of the emotion. The distinc-tion comes from Stoic thought, but some Church Fathers use it. And later, St. Thomas Aquinas also mentions the distinction, citing Saint Jerome's comments about it. Again, the distinction is between the first stirring of the emotion and its subsequent stirring or urging. The first stirring is the first movement of the emotion; it is called a *pro-passion* or *proto-passion* from the Greek *propatheia*.

The reason for thinking about this distinction was to un-derstand what is morally ideal for human beings. Is the morally perfect person not moved at all by emotions? Even if some of the Stoics argued something like this, early Christian thinkers rejected it. How could they say that the morally perfect person is never affected by emotions? After all, Jesus himself felt sorrow to the point of weeping, and He was angry when He overturned the tables in the Temple area. No, the morally perfect person — namely, Jesus — *is* moved by emotions.

But still, the early Christian thinkers realized that it was not good to be *ruled* by our emotions. A morally perfect person would not do things *simply* out of anger or fear or sorrow. Rath-er, reason has to see that the action is right and give its consent.

Emotions have their role, but reason should have a governing role. Reason, after all, is like the charioteer guiding the horses. So it was with Christ. His reason always maintained its governing role with respect to the emotions. It was always in the driver's seat. So, when He felt anger, it was still under the leadership of right reason. Anger did not take over, leading Him to act *simply* out of anger.

When ancient thinkers speak about the first stirrings of an emotion, they mean the experience of emotion that is still under the control of reason. But the subsequent urging by the emotion that they speak of is when the emotion rebels against reason's governing role. It develops into something unruly, and it challenges the control held by reason. The more successful this challenge to the rule of reason, the more the emotion pushes reason aside and takes over the reins — that is, the more the emotion domineers over the mind.

Notice that the problem here is not that the emotion becomes intense. The intensity of the emotion is not itself the issue. As long as the emotion is integrated with the mind, and thus cooperates with the mind's leadership, having a deeply and strongly felt emotion is not a problem. It may even be a benefit. So, the problem is not that one feels an emotion deeply and strongly. Rather, the problem is that the force of the emotion works against the mind. The emotion wants to be in control instead of the mind.

So, when first experienced, the emotion is not rebelling against the control held by reason, but when subsequently experienced, it is. Notice that the first experience may or may not be in accord with reason. That is to say, it may be a rightly ordered emotion that is urging us to act correctly, or it may not be. Yet, even when it is not rightly ordered, it does not try to overthrow reason. It urges reason to consent to a wrong action, but reason maintains control of the reins. Thus, I may have a disordered fear.

Let us say that it is disordered because it is based on an imagined danger, not a real one. The first experience of this emotion urges me to act wrongly, but my reason is still in control. My fear is not working to push reason aside.

The second or subsequent experience of the emotion, however, is different. Now the emotion is pushing reason out of the driver's seat. And notice that this second phase or experience of an emotion can occur even when the first experience was rightly ordered! So, if I originally had a good and healthy fear that has been urging me to take proper precautions in some matter, it can still become panicky and try to take control from reason. The first experience of the fear was right, but the second experience, which is always wrong, still developed.

Christ did not have this subsequent experience of emotions. None of His emotions rebelled against His mind and tried to take over. He felt the emotions, to be sure, but they did not work against His reason. And what is more, His first experience of an emotion was always rightly ordered. He never had a disordered emotion in the first place. Rather, in Him existed the perfect integration of mind and emotions.

Obviously, the situation is different with us. Our first experience of an emotion can be disordered, and even when it is not, the subsequent experience can occur and cause problems. In this chapter, we have been considering cases in which the emotion is wrong when it first arises. Whether it is fear, anger, desire, or another emotion, even in its first experience, it is pushing us to act wrongly. But at first, reason has the reins and is in control. The situation can change, however. The emotion can subsequently become overwhelming. Reason starts to lose control. It becomes like a charioteer losing control of his horses, and so they, not he, are dictating the direction. When this subsequent situation arises, then we have the step that I am calling "domineering emotion."

In the steps to action, the first experience of the emotion is what I am simply calling "emotion." After it, the additional step of the domineering emotion can occur. It does not always occur, and a person can surely do a bad action without it. Thus, the man exiting the airplane can simply consent to his desire to take the wallet that was left behind, without that desire ever developing into a domineering emotion. But when a domineering emotion does arise, avoiding the wrong action that is being urged becomes especially difficult.

"Craving" an Addictive Behavior

When addiction counselors speak of this step, which I am calling "domineering emotion," they are especially speaking of the emotion of desire for an addictive behavior. This experience of desire is sometimes called "craving." The desire for the addictive behavior becomes very, very hard to resist. Right thinking loses control or is on the verge of losing control of the situation. In fact, reason is put into the service of the craving, coming up with rationalizations for satisfying it and finding ways to do so.

There are even structural changes in the brain that occur as an addiction develops, and that help to explain this experience of craving. The parts of the brain used for controlling behaviors become less able to support a person in saying no to the desire. So, when the emotion of desire moves into the craving stage, the emotional urging is extremely hard to resist. The emotional push for the addictive behavior practically takes over. Again, one rationalizes, makes excuses, and even thinks of more tempting thoughts. If one tries to brush the tempting thoughts away, they keep coming, and the emotional urging keeps pushing one strongly toward the bad behavior.

Is this craving the same as what ancient thinkers meant by that subsequent urging of an emotion that works to overthrow the mind? I do not think they are exactly the same. For one, when an emotion rebels against reason, this can happen to varying degrees, whereas this craving is when the rebellion is at an especially high degree. Still, there is an interesting parallel between what the ancient thinkers discussed and what contemporary addiction counselors speak of. They both indicate that an emotion can reach a phase when it starts to take control of a person. The emotion takes on an overwhelming quality. When this happens, whether with an addiction or a habitual sin, we can speak of a domineering emotion as another step in the series of steps that lead to an unwanted action.

Needless to say, we want to resist the emotion in its initial phase, before it becomes domineering. Remember, having the first stirrings of a misguided emotion is not something to beat ourselves up about. Those stirrings happen as bad thoughts pop into our heads. Often, the bad thoughts simply arise in our minds without our willing them, and they lead to these first stirrings of the emotion. This can happen without any culpability on our part. But we must try to nip those thoughts in the bud and not let them blossom into something more. Sometimes we can rebuke a thought so that it goes away. This would be an instance of a healthy anger directed toward sinful temptations, as discussed in chapter 4. At other times, we simply try to get the thoughts out of our minds or to ignore them. To do this, it can be helpful to do get our minds on something else, whether by reading a book or reading Scripture or taking up some distracting activity that is morally permissible. Still, at other times, we may need to weaken a bad thought by seeing how it is a misguided attempt to meet a genuine need while also building up a counteracting correct thought about how to meet that need. This is discussed in the next chapter.

If we do not resist the thoughts that are prompting a wayward emotion, the emotion may become domineering. It can develop to such a point that it begins to take over. Again, the experience is like that of a charioteer who loses control of his horses, and the horses run recklessly with him in tow.

How to Break from a Domineering Emotion

How does one resist the urging of an emotion when it becomes so overwhelming? How does someone in that situation not do the bad action? It is possible, as some people have shown, but it is very hard. Here are a few things to do in order to fight a domineering emotion — whether the emotion is urging us to anger, lust, jealousy, discouragement, or some other thing. You will see that all these helps are familiar to us already, but it can be good to remind ourselves of them.

First and foremost, pray to God. The fight against habitual sin is a spiritual battle, and we need God's help. Even in cases of clinical addiction, it is a spiritual battle as well as a physiological one. Thus, in twelve-step addiction-recovery programs, one is told to rely on a higher power. So, keep praying. And it is also important to ask Our Lady for help. Our mother in heaven is a valuable intercessor for us.

Second, depending on the situation, self-denial can help. Denying ourselves certain comforts or gratifications can weaken the greediness of our emotions. This can give us a little more leverage in the battle, and all the help we can get is appreciated. But we also need good judgment. Certain kinds of self-denial can make things worse. Remember, being hungry or tired can sometimes work as a trigger! Still, there are cases when self-denial helps.

The third thing is what the monastic tradition calls "disclosure of thoughts." Being able to speak about the bad behavior out loud to a spiritual director or simply to a confessor is valuable, even though this can be difficult to do. We have here another convergence between our spiritual tradition and addiction counseling. A sort of disclosure of thoughts is part of twelve-step recovery programs. Whether it is to a counselor, a support group, or to a sponsor, talking about the behavior out loud helps to reduce its control over us.

There is a nice story about this in the *Sayings of the Desert Fathers*, an ancient collection of stories and sayings from the early monks of Egypt. Abba Serapion says that when he was young and under the tutelage of Abba Theonas, he began to steal food and eat it secretly. He goes on to describe this as follows: "For some time I went on with this, until the sin began to dominate my mind, and I could not stop myself." This may not be an addiction, but it seems to have become a habitual sin. Serapion certainly seems to have experienced a domineering emotion, since his desire for the food became so overwhelming that it "dominated" his mind! Now, Abba Theonas did not know what Serapion was doing, but one day Theonas spoke to others about the importance of not concealing their thoughts from their spiritual father. Hearing this, Serapion was moved to confess to Theonas. Theonas replied: "My son, you are set free from your captivity without my saying anything. You are freed by your own confession." Disclosing our sinful thoughts and bad actions to a spiritual director or in confession remains valuable.

May the Lord set us free from any habitual sin and anything else that holds us back on the journey to the kingdom.

....

Glory be to the Father and to the Son and to the Holy Spirit; as it was in the beginning, is now, and ever shall be, world without end. Amen.

CHAPTER 8

Persuading the Emotions

.... **PRAYER** ....

Give us, Lord, the freedom that You promise so that we can
be free from any captivity to sin. May we run the path of
Your commands with joyful hearts, and may we be faithful
workers who know the delight of virtue. Through Christ our
Lord. Amen.

....

When I spoke in the last chapter about the steps leading to an action, I left something out. It is something that addiction counselors also see as a step — or rather, it is not so much a step as something in the background of a bad behavior. This thing is already present when the progression of steps begins with a trigger. Indeed, it is why the series of steps begins in the first place. I am speaking of an unmet need.

In counseling, unmet needs are sometimes identified as being at the bottom of problematic behavior. The behavior is the result, or partly the result, of trying to meet a fundamental need in the wrong way. We may understand a "need" here as something that is necessary for human fulfillment. For example, consider the need to think well of oneself. We may call it self-esteem or a positive self-image. Whatever we call it, it is a genuine need for fulfillment. Without thinking well of oneself, one cannot be fulfilled and happy. Rather, one is miserable.

But how do we strive to meet this need? Here is one way: We put other people down so that, in comparison with them, we think well of ourselves. Thus, we have tried to meet a genuine need, but in a wrong way. Notice that trying to meet the need is not wrong. We can't help but pursue a need for fulfillment. As I said before, we naturally strive after what will bring us fulfillment, and these needs are required for that fulfillment. So, it is not an option just to disregard the need. But how do we go about meeting the need? What are right ways for meeting the need? Those will be good actions. As for the wrong ways, they are bad actions.

Consider another need for fulfillment to illustrate this further. It is what psychological counselors call "intimacy needs." Today, the word *intimacy* is often taken to mean physical intimacy — that is, sexual relations. But the original meaning of *intimacy* was not restricted to sexual matters, and here the need for intimacy means the need for close relationships with others. In the case of marriage, the close relationship will involve physical intimacy as part of it, but in other relationships it will not, or at least should not, involve this.

All of us have this need for close relationships with others. Again, the question is not whether we should try to meet the need. The question is how to go about meeting it. Will we do so correctly or incorrectly? The correct ways of trying to meet the need are good actions, and the incorrect ways are bad actions.

Suppose I try to meet this need as follows. When I encounter someone I would like to be friends with, I try to impress that person by telling little lies about myself. I try to look better than I am in certain areas. Obviously, this is not a correct way to meet the need for a close relationship, and thus it is not a good action. But if I go about trying to be friends with this person in correct ways, those actions are good actions.

Where does this leave us with regard to the steps to action? Now we have something that precedes these steps: an unmet need. This need is why the series of steps begins in the first place. The steps arise and lead one toward an action in order to satisfy the need or to help toward that end.

We all have various unmet needs, since we are not yet perfectly fulfilled. And, as just mentioned, we cannot help but seek to meet these needs. But to be more precise, it is not as if an unmet need is constantly prompting us to satisfy it. Often an unmet need lies dormant and does not make itself felt. In that case, we are not being prompted to meet the need. Over the course of our lives, however, something will happen to wake up the dormant unmet need. In other words, something occurs that makes us sense that we are not fulfilled with regard to that need. That occurrence is the trigger that leads to a thought about how to meet the need. And so begins the series of steps: A trigger leads to a thought, which prompts an emotion, which may become a domineering emotion, but even if not, it urges an action that is considered conducive to meeting the need.

For example, I might meet a very impressive person, and that encounter makes me feel inadequate in comparison. This encounter is the trigger that wakes up the unmet need that had been sleeping within me. Here, the unmet need is the need to think well of myself. The encounter with the impressive person and my resulting sense of inadequacy wake up this need, and like a baby awakened from sleep, it cries out for what will satisfy it. So, now I form a thought about how to meet the need. And as noted, I might form a bad thought, such as the idea that, by putting others down, I will think well about myself in comparison. But whether a good or bad thought is formed, it is by means of the trigger that the unmet need leads to a thought, and that thought leads to an emotion, which urges an action.

The Critical Role of Thoughts

Notice that the thought is crucial. It is about how the need will be met. If I form a bad thought about this, it will give rise to a misguided emotion, which urges a bad action. But if I form a correct thought about how to meet the need, then the thought will give rise to a rightly directed emotion, which urges me toward a good action.

This, then, is the key to cultivating the right emotions, the ones that will support us in doing good. By forming correct thoughts about how our authentic needs are met, the mind causes the right emotions to arise. Recall that the mind cannot simply tell an emotion to arise or to go away. Thoughts are what lead to the emotions (and they do so, as noted in the previous chapter, because perceptions are in them). So, if the mind is going to foster the right emotions, it must form correct thoughts about how authentic needs are met.

This is what I mean by saying we must persuade the emotions. I have said that the mind governs the emotions in two ways. In the first, it withholds its consent from the wayward emotions that are urging the wrong actions. I spoke about this especially in the previous chapter. But the other way is by persuading the emotions.

This persuading is what Aristotle was getting at when he said that we rule the emotions in a "political" way. When dealing with a free citizenry, a civic leader must put thoughts before the people in order to persuade them. The leader cannot simply tell the people what to do. Likewise, the mind needs to put thoughts before the emotional part of the soul in order to persuade it. The emotional part wants our needs met, since this brings joy. So, the mind must put before it thoughts about how the needs are met, thoughts that, in effect, say, "Look, here is how you meet the need so as to find joy."

When the thoughts about how to meet a need are correct, they persuade the emotional part to have the right emotions. But as we will see later, forming correct thoughts has its challenges.

Clarifications about Needs

I should say some more about the needs for human fulfillment, in order to avoid confusion. Yet there is so much to be said on this topic that I would like to write a book on it, to pick up where this one leaves off. It is not possible to give a full treatment of our needs in this book, but here are a few points to make sure we are understanding the needs as intended.

Many have heard of the hierarchy of needs proposed by the American psychologist Abraham Maslow. I am not, however, speaking of needs in the same way. I think there is some overlap, but there are important differences. First, Maslow was not writing from a theological perspective, whereas I am. He does not include God in his hierarchy, but the view of the needs that I am presenting here centers on God.

In fact, in the final analysis, God is the one thing needed (see Lk 10:42). And this can be shown through a simple argument. Note that anything we genuinely need is a good thing. Next, note that all good things are found in God most perfectly — that is, in an infinite, preeminent way. Therefore, all the good things we need for fulfillment are found preeminently in God, and when we attain perfect union with God in heaven, we will have all those things so that all our needs will be met.

This is not to say that there will be nothing else that we enjoy in heaven besides God. We will enjoy, for instance, the presence of the holy angels and the saints, in whose company will be loved ones from our lives on earth. But we will enjoy them in God, and it is our enjoyment of God that will make us fully alive and fulfilled. This perfect joy — a joy that we cannot fully imagine (see 1 Cor 2:9) — is the ultimate goal toward which we are journeying while on earth.

But we are not there yet. We are not yet perfectly united with God as we will be in heaven, so as to have all good things in Him. And since we are not there yet, a few important points follow.

For one, we will not have all our needs met here on earth. If all our needs for fulfillment were met on earth, we would be perfectly happy on earth, but again, such happiness comes only in heaven, when we will have perfect union with God. So, while we journey to God, we will have sorrows from being frustrated in our striving to fulfill certain needs.

This leads to a second point. Maslow maintained that if we were frustrated in meeting lower needs, that would keep us from being able to rise up to attain higher needs. This can be true in some cases, but it is not necessarily true. Consider the need for bodily health, which Maslow also recognized, and consider the need to be lovingly attentive to God and to think about Him, which Maslow did not recognize. We may call this latter need the need to be mindful of God. The first — having bodily health — is a lower need than the second — being mindful of God. But even those who are suffering an illness that prevents them from meeting the need for bodily health can be mindful of God. In fact, sometimes those who are suffering an illness are especially mindful of God.

So, the frustration of a lower need does not always prevent people from meeting a higher need. If that were always the case, then we would always have to meet lower needs before we met higher ones. But in fact, our faith indicates that it often works in reverse. For instance, the martyrs allowed themselves to suffer the complete loss of bodily health, but they remained mindful of God. Yet, at the resurrection, they will receive their bodies back in perfect health. First, they fulfilled the higher need of being mindful of God, and as a result, they will later have the lower need of bodily health fulfilled.

Furthermore, our needs are an important way in which God leads us to himself. There are many things that God has done or continues to do to lead us to the enjoyment of himself, such as the sending of His Son; the gifts of the Church, Scripture, and the sacraments; and His active presence in our lives through the graces He gives. Alongside all these marvelous ways, and preceding them, is how He made us.

God made us with these needs, and He made the good things that can satisfy our needs. When, according to God's design, we search out and attain the correct things to meet a need, we experience a wholesome joy. That wholesome joy is a foretaste of the perfect joy we will have when we attain God in heaven. For example, when I truly meet the need for a close relationship with another, such as by having a true friend, the joy in this is a foretaste of the joy that will come from sitting with the Lord and His holy ones at the table in the kingdom.

So, the joys that come from correctly meeting our needs on earth lead us on to that perfect joy in heaven. They are hints of the indescribable goodness of God that we will fully enjoy in the next life. Thus, we are encouraged to keep moving on the journey to God. Yes, as noted a moment ago, not all our needs will be met on earth, and so we will have sorrows. But as described in chapter 5, our sorrows can also help us on the journey to God. They remind us that we have not reached our goal of fulfillment in God, and they motivate us to do things to resolve this problem. Therefore, both the joys from meeting our needs and the sorrows from not meeting them help us on the journey.

Of course, I am speaking about authentic needs for fulfillment — the things without which one could not be perfectly fulfilled. They are the essentials for fulfillment. Some were mentioned in the last part of chapter 6 — namely, bodily health, right treatment from those around us, and the avoidance of sin. Sometimes, however, we think we need things that we do not really need. So, we can be mistaken in that way. The monk discussed in chapter 6, for example, wrongly thought that he needed to be the abbot in order to be happy. To avoid this mistake, we might ask, "What are the authentic needs for fulfillment?"

In fact, having a list of our genuine needs is helpful, and for our present discussion, I would like to offer a list of five needs. Please note that this is not the only list we can come up with. When we consider what human fulfillment looks like, we can parse this in different ways, so as to come up with different lists of authentic needs. Also note that, since I am giving only a brief account of the needs here, this list of five needs is far from exhaustive. But it does cover some of the most important needs. They are: the need for bodily health, the need to think well of oneself, the need for close relationships, the need for moral integrity, and the need to be mindful of God.

Four of the five have already been mentioned in the examples above. The new one is the need for moral integrity. It is the need to follow what is right and just. God is good and upright (Ps 25:8), and in order to be close to God, in whom is our ultimate fulfillment, we must be good and upright. So, avoiding sin and being morally upright are needed for fulfillment.

Two final points of clarification: First, I am not saying that we are sufficient by ourselves to meet our needs. Rather, none of us can do this on his or her own. For one thing, we have a need for close relationships with others, and these are a two-way street. Yes, I must do my part, but so must the other, if we are to have a close relationship. Even more importantly, the meeting of our needs requires God's help. God wants us to meet our needs in order to come closer to Him, and this requires the help of His grace. As noted at the end of chapter 6, we should despair of the idea that we are self-sufficient in our journey to God.

Second, meeting our needs is not a self-centered project. Again, we can think of the need for close relationships with others. Meeting this need is incompatible with pursuing our needs in a way that ignores other people or uses them for selfish purposes. Also, to be self-centered works against the need for moral integrity. The morally upright person loves his neighbor as himself. If we live selfishly, we fail to meet this need, and we distance ourselves from God, our ultimate fulfillment.

Retrieving a Traditional Perspective on Morality

In speaking about trying to meet our needs in the correct ways, we are returning to a traditional Catholic view of morality. In this view — held by such notables as Saints Augustine and Thomas Aquinas — the final aim of living a good, morally upright life is to attain the happiness promised by God. God made us for true happiness, and He promises to lead us to it.

I mentioned this happiness or fulfillment in the preceding chapters. On the one hand, we cannot help but strive after it, and thus we all seek it. But on the other hand, people understand it differently, so they seek after different versions of happiness. One can understand it as some superficial happiness, but that is not meant here. Or one can understand it simply as feeling good in both superficial and deep ways, but it is only about the feelings. There is no spiritual dimension having to do with God. That is also not meant here. Yes, full and complete happiness will entail feelings, for it will encompass the feeling part of the soul as well as the thinking part. It is to be fully alive in all the parts of the soul. But it is principally a spiritual happiness from union with God, and this spiritual happiness is so wonderful that, as indicated in chapter 2, it "overflows" into the feeling part.

If we stay true to God, then, even while on earth, we experience some of this happiness. We get glimpses of it. But its full realization will be in the next life. The Latin word for this happiness is *beatitudo,* from which we get the term *beatitude,* as in the Beatitudes (see Mt 5:1–12). When Jesus says, "Blessed are the poor in spirit," and so on, He is saying that the people who fulfill the Beatitudes are truly happy, for they will be fully happy in the life to come. The Latin word *beatitudo* is also connected to the phrase *beatific vision,* that direct, face-to-face vision of God in the life to come. To have that vision is to be perfectly united to God in love, and the joy of that union will overflow into every crevice of our being, so we will be fully happy.

This is what we are striving for on the journey to the kingdom. God is leading us there, and in turn, we must cooperate by how we act. This cooperation is the moral life. But part of this cooperation is, as just noted, getting a correct understanding in our minds of the happiness we seek. It is not a superficial happiness nor just about feelings. It is the fulfillment that comes from God and encompasses the soul.

I have been talking about our needs to help us in this task of thinking correctly about fulfillment. We want to reflect on these questions: "What are our needs for fulfillment? And how are they met?" Again, when we form correct thoughts about how authentic needs are met, this persuades our emotions to push and pull us in the right directions.

Recall that thoughts lead to emotions because they have perceptions within them. And so, when we work at forming correct thoughts about fulfillment, we are working at forming correct perceptions. This explains why forming correct thoughts can be difficult.

As mentioned in the introduction, perceptions can be hidden and persistent. I can experience an emotion, but the underlying perception might not be clear. And even if it is clear, and I see that it is wrong, still it can persist. Therefore, as we form correct thoughts with correct perceptions, we should not be surprised if incorrect perceptions persist, so that we continue to have bad thoughts.

What we experience, in other words, are conflicting perceptions (and thus conflicting thoughts). We are cultivating the right perceptions within our thoughts, but wrong perceptions push back and will not go away quietly. And since the incorrect perceptions linger, they lead to errant emotions. Thus, even when we form good perceptions that lead to good emotions, errant emotions can still be felt and may even be felt very strongly.

Consider again the example of telling lies about myself in order to make a friend and to meet the need for close relationships. If this is happening, I am experiencing the emotion of desire to tell such lies. And behind this emotion is an incorrect perception. To identify the perception, it helps to consider the emotion of liking beneath the desire and to see the perception behind the liking. The emotion of liking, we recall, is based on the perception that something is agreeable to me. What am I perceiving as agreeable in this case? It is for the potential friend to like me based on a lie. That is the incorrect perception.

But where did this incorrect perception come from? The origins of our perceptions can be mysterious. Perceptions can come from explicit thinking — that is, from thinking something "out loud" in our heads — but they do not always do so, or they only partially do so. Thus, when we know that a perception is wrong and yet it persists, we find that it is being sustained by something other than clear, explicit thinking. What sustains the perception may be, for example, habitual associations, past experiences, or attachments, or a combination of these. And sometimes we cannot identify what is sustaining the perception.

But suppose in the present example that I come to see that my incorrect perception is based on a kind of desperation. I do not believe that I can get people to like me as I truly am but only if I make up things about myself. That is, I have the view that making a friend is hopeless if I let a person see me as I truly am. This view is not thought "out loud" in my head, and yet it is at work in my soul. And it leads to the persistence of this incorrect perception, even though I know that it is wrong.

To combat this perception and the emotions it generates, I need to form an alternative and correct perception on the matter. Thus, I may consider that a true friend is one who likes me for who I truly am. That friend sees the inherent goodness I have as a human being and the unique instantiation of that goodness in my particular case. The friend will be aware of my faults but will not reduce me to them. Rather, my friend will want me to overcome them so that my genuine goodness will shine forth more clearly.

With such considerations I form a new and correct perception. Now I perceive that having this kind of friend, a true friend who likes me for my true self, is agreeable. This is what I like and desire, and in turn, I have a disliking and aversion toward the prospect of having a friend who likes me based on a lie, since that would frustrate my desire for a true friend. Also, the new perception leads to the desire to do the things that would lead to having such a friend, such as sharing true things about myself as the relationship with a potential friend develops over time.

And yet, as I maintain this new perception, the old one does not go away. It keeps urging me to lie about myself, and this conflicts with the desire to gradually disclose my true self. Keeping the new perception in the forefront is difficult. Even as I try to do so, I may occasionally give in to the old perception and tell a lie about myself. If I am not careful, the old perception may even lead me to give up on the new perception. I might end up thinking, "Sure, it would be nice to have such a friend, but it is pie-in-the-sky thinking. It is unrealistic."

So, there is this conflict within me between these two perceptions and the emotions they generate. To borrow an example we considered in chapter 2, this conflict is not unlike the lactose-intolerant person who is conflicted between liking and disliking ice cream. But in that case, both of the underlying perceptions are correct. Eating the ice cream is agreeable to the person's *taste*, and not eating it is agreeable to the person's *digestion*. In the present case of wanting to make a friend, though, one of the perceptions is wrong. Still, it will not go away, but it lingers and works against the correct perception I am trying to cultivate.

Making Perceptions More Convincing

In this present life, we cannot escape such conflicts within us. Incorrect perceptions will linger and tempt us. Still, we want to help the correct perception to prevail so that it will influence us more than the incorrect perception. This means making the new perception more convincing. We want it to become more "real," as it were, to the emotional part of the soul. Then it will give rise to a stronger emotion that will more effectively counteract the errant emotion that is resulting from the incorrect perception.

We know from experience what an unconvincing perception looks like. It remains too exclusively in the mind and not enough in the feeling part of the soul. At this point, some would understand me to be saying that the perception needs to move from the mind to the heart. But although that can be OK to say, I avoid it for two reasons. First, what I mean by the feeling or emotional part of the soul is not the heart. I would, instead, describe the heart as where the mind and the feeling part intersect. Second, it is not that the perception needs to move out of the mind and into the feeling part, as if it should be in one or the other. Having the perception in the mind is not the problem. The problem is that it is not *also* in the feeling part. To make a perception more convincing is to make it more felt in the emotional part of the soul, so that a stronger emotion arises from it.

To achieve this, we need to confirm the perception, and

three things that especially confirm a perception are experiences, examples, and teachings. They make it more "real" and convincing to the emotional part of the soul. I will give instances of this below. We should note, however, that if any of these things is going to confirm a perception, we have to think about it in the right way. We have to consider the experience, example, or teaching aright, as the following examples will show.

We easily recognize that experiences can confirm a perception. Suppose I have experienced a true friendship in which my friend likes me for my true self. Then I know from experience the joy that this brings, and that confirms my perception that it is agreeable to have someone like me as I truly am. The perception becomes more "real," more convincing, and thus it generates stronger emotions to support the correct way of meeting the need for close relationships.

Experience can also confirm an incorrect perception, however, *unless* we think about it correctly. Suppose, for instance, that I tried to share things about myself with another person in the interest of cultivating a friendship with that person. Things seemed to be going well, but then the other made fun of me about something personal that I shared. Obviously, this is hurtful. And in turn, the experience can make me think that it is more agreeable to keep my thoughts to myself than to share them. And so, an incorrect perception is confirmed, and not a correct perception, about how the need for a close relationship is met.

To avoid this, we must consider the matter aright. So, given that this experience was painful, I might recall some of the things said about sorrow in chapter 5. For instance, sorrow makes us aware of a problem and motivates us to diagnose its cause so that the problem might be resolved. The problem is that I failed to attain true friendship. What is the cause? It is not that I tried to make a true friend by sharing things about myself but that the potential friend made fun of what I shared. In fact, trying to make a true friend by sharing things about myself was the right and, indeed, courageous thing to do. So, I should not blame myself that it didn't work out. Perhaps I shared things about myself too quickly, before letting the relationship develop and seeing that this was a person I could trust. If so, that was part of what caused the problem, and I can learn from the experience to be more discerning in the future about what to share and when. But even so, the primary cause of the problem is how the other acted.

When I consider the matter aright by, in this case, correctly diagnosing the cause of the pain, the experience actually confirms a correct perception. Then, when my pain deepens my disliking, the deepened disliking is especially directed at how the potential friend acted. So, I have the strong and correct perception that this person's insensitivity toward what I shared is disagreeable. Such insensitivity is bad, and it gets in the way of forming a true friendship. With this correct perception, confirmed by my painful experience, I am now motivated to avoid encountering that behavior in the future and to avoid ever acting that way toward another.

Likewise, examples can also help confirm correct perceptions, insofar as we consider them aright. The examples may be fictional or from real life. Fictional examples can be convincing when they are plausible, but real-life examples are especially convincing. But again, how we consider the examples is crucial. For example, the examples of the martyrs confirm multiple correct perceptions that we have as Christians, such as the perception that the total self-giving love of the martyrs toward God is something beautiful (see Ps 116:15) and that God rewards His faithful servants by taking them to himself in heaven (Wis 3:1). But others might consider the suffering and death of the martyrs differently. They may look at what happened to the martyrs and think, "That only shows that trying to do the right thing doesn't pay off. It can get you killed." So, if an example is going to confirm a correct perception, it must be thought about correctly. And when that is done, examples help.

Finally, there are teachings. Consider this teaching from the Book of Sirach: "A faithful friend is a sturdy shelter: / he that has found one has found a treasure" (6:14). This confirms the correct perception that true friendship is agreeable. It notes how a true friend is a treasure and, like all treasures, is to be prized and not taken for granted. But as with experiences and examples, one must consider the teaching correctly. Someone can consider this teaching and conclude that, like a treasure, a true friend is not easily found and that the effort to find such a friend is not worth it.

Delayed Gratification

So, one challenge to persuading the emotions is the resistance offered by incorrect perceptions that linger. This creates conflict within us, as noted. But another challenge arises when two correct perceptions are in conflict within us. This is the case of the lactose-intolerant person who has two correct perceptions that are in conflict. One cannot follow the emotions that stem from both perceptions but must choose one perception and its emotion over the other.

For example, consider the conflict between two correct perceptions that a firefighter experiences when risking his health, if not his life, in order to rescue someone from a burning building. Let us say he sees that he is very likely to suffer burns, if not be killed, by attempting the rescue. But the rescue has a decent chance of success. He has two competing perceptions, and both are correct. He naturally has the perception that staying out of the burning building is an agreeable thing to do. But he also has the perception that fulfilling his duty by attempting to rescue the person in the building is an agreeable thing to do.

Here is a situation in which only one perception can be

followed. Which one? As difficult as it is, he should attempt to rescue the person in the building. That is, he should follow the perception that attempting the rescue is an agreeable thing to do. Indeed, he perceives that this is *the* agreeable thing to do in the situation. It trumps what the other perception would have him do.

This can be explained in terms of the needs for fulfillment. By entering the burning building to rescue someone, the firefighter is meeting the need for moral integrity. Indeed, if he neglected his duty, he would not meet this need. True, this means that he must forgo or put at risk being able to meet the need for bodily health. Yet this is the right thing to do, since the need for integrity is a higher need than bodily health. It can never be sacrificed — that is, one should never act against moral integrity — in order to meet another need.

As noted before, moral integrity is necessary for remaining close to God, in whom our ultimate fulfillment is found. So, we must never try to meet another need, even though the other need is an authentic need, by doing what is morally wrong. That would separate us from God, which never helps. Never doing what is morally wrong does not mean that one must always do a heroic thing. The firefighter, however, must do the heroic act, since he committed himself to this duty. An onlooker at the scene of the fire would not necessarily be obliged to attempt the rescue, and so that person would not necessarily be acting against moral integrity by not attempting it. Still, we should never act against moral integrity, even in the attempt to meet another authentic need.

The same applies to the need to be mindful of God, given that this need, too, is necessary for remaining close to God. There is no other need for which we should forgo this need. This mindfulness does not mean that we never stop thinking explicitly of God. If that were so, we would fail to meet this need when we went to sleep. Rather, meeting this need means that we think directly about God now and again, and at other times we remain mindful of God in the sense that whatever we are doing is directed to what pleases Him. This and the need for moral integrity work together to keep us close to God, and there is never a justifiable reason to turn away from God.

Notice that cases like that of the firefighter are like the cases mentioned toward the end of chapter 6, in that something essential for fulfillment is not being attained. To meet a higher need for fulfillment, one forgoes meeting another need. Thus, the firefighter forgoes preserving his bodily health to meet the higher need for moral integrity. In chapter 6, we noted that we never lose hope for our fulfillment in God. So, even when one forgoes meeting a lower need for fulfillment, one still hopes that God will fulfill the lower need eventually — in heaven, if not earlier. So, the firefighter who sustains lifelong injuries hopes to regain full health in the next life. And the person who loses friends by doing what is right hopes to gain true and lasting friends in the next life, if not later in this life. But to satisfy these needs eventually, we must continue to meet the need for moral integrity and the need for mindfulness of God. As we saw in chapter 6, carrying out the critical means for fulfillment ensures that we meet these two most important needs.

Thus, some lower needs are delayed in their gratification. The time before such needs are gratified is burdensome, and to bear this burden well, we need God's grace — which often works through the support of others. Such times put our faith to the test. God has promised that in the next life, all our needs will be met and we will be perfectly happy, more than we can imagine. But do we believe this? Other thoughts pop into our heads and discourage us.

Here, too, we can look to teachings (especially from Scripture), examples (especially those of Christ and the saints), and experiences (especially our own experiences of God's previous presence and help in our lives). Such teachings, examples, and experiences can confirm correct thinking about the matter so that our emotions will support us through the trial.

Conclusion

To see our journey to God in terms of meeting our needs is a positive approach to the moral life and to converting our emotions. As just shown, this is not easy. But it is a positive approach that is full of hope for God's kingdom and hope in God's mercy.

To encourage us further, allow me to note that there is another need, other than the need for moral integrity and the need for mindfulness of God, that we should never forgo. This need is never in conflict with other needs so that we would need to forgo it in order to meet another need. It is the need to think well of ourselves.

You are made in the image of God, and that gives you more value than you realize. It means that you have the potential to share in the very life of God, and there is no greater potential that a creature can have. Whether you have been journeying to God or have turned away from Him, you have this great dignity. Be encouraged, then. Experience the wholesome joy of meeting this need by accepting your worth, and let that joy draw you to the kingdom of the Father.

....

Glory be to the Father and to the Son and to the Holy Spirit; as it was in the beginning, is now, and ever shall be, world without end. Amen.

Acknowledgments

There are very many people whom I should thank for helping and supporting me in writing this book. I cannot mention them all, but here are some to whom I especially owe my thanks.

First, I want to thank my monastery, St. Procopius Abbey, for the opportunities to study these topics and for being one of the audiences with whom I worked out my ideas about the emotions as I gave talks on them. In that regard, I also want to thank the various monasteries to whom I gave the talks that developed into this book: Belmont Abbey (Belmont, North Carolina), St. Mary's Abbey (Morristown, New Jersey), St. Walburga Monastery (Elizabeth, New Jersey), Portsmouth Abbey (Portsmouth, Rhode Island), St. Joseph Abbey (Covington, Louisiana), New Melleray Abbey (Peosta, Iowa), St. Scholastica Priory and St. Mary's Monastery (Petersham, Massachusetts), St. Gregory's Abbey (Shawnee, Oklahoma), and Marmion Abbey (Aurora, Illinois). My gratitude also goes to some of the employees at St. Procopius Abbey with whom I had many conversations about the emotions, especially Jeanine Jelinek and Gwen Sanborn. Those conversations helped me to think through the topic further and to find clearer ways to speak about the emotions.

I also want to thank Fr. Andrew Hofer, OP; Abbot Lawrence Stasyszen, OSB; Abbot Placid Solari, OSB; and Abbot Mark

Scott, OCSO. They helped me in different ways, sometimes unknown to them, in producing this book. I am also grateful to the editors at Our Sunday Visitor for their indispensable help and support — namely, Mary Beth Giltner, whose editing improved this book, as well as Rebecca Martin, Scott Richert, and Fr. Patrick Briscoe, OP. Any errors remain mine alone.

A final thanks to the monks of St. Benedict's Abbey in Atchison, Kansas, where I lived as I finished this book. I am grateful for their hospitality, prayers, and support.

APPENDIX

A Study Guide

This appendix is meant as a brief study guide to help individual readers or study groups to think through the emotions as they are understood in this book. It may be used before or after reading the chapters in the book. After each section, there are study exercises to facilitate comprehension. Also, this appendix includes some material not in the book, including one emotion — namely, the emotion of daring.

Section 1: What an Emotion Is and Its Elements

We start with the observation that we respond to objects on two basic levels. The introduction mentions the example of a homeless man with a bad odor. On one level, you want to help the man as a fellow human being; on the other, you want to run from him due to the odor. Another example is someone with a revolting illness. On one level, you want to tend to the person, and on the other, you want to get away from the person's illness. The first level of response is a free choice based on the mind's reasoning. The other level is not so much a free response as a felt reaction.

This second kind of response is an emotion. Thus, we define an emotion as a *felt reaction*. As a *reaction*, it is a response to some object. The object prompts the reaction within you. It moves you. Also, the reaction is *felt*. That is, it is a physiological response rather than a mental one. Sometimes the physiological reaction is strong, sometimes only subtle. Sometimes it is felt superficially, at other times very deeply.

While an object prompts the felt reaction in you, it does so through the perception you form of it. The introduction gives the example of children reacting differently to Santa Claus in a shopping mall. Some children perceive him as a friendly person and are attracted to him, while others perceive him as scary and are afraid of him. There are different reactions to the same object because there are different perceptions of that object. A similar thing happens with a clown: Some people perceive the clown as funny, others as menacing. In turn, they have different felt reactions — that is, emotions — toward the clown. So, if the same object prompts different emotions, it cannot simply be the object that prompts an emotion, but the object *as you perceive it* that does so. In other words, how you look at something determines the emotion you will have in response to that thing.

So, with every emotion, there are two elements to consider: your perception of some object and the reaction you feel toward the object. The second is the emotion itself, but the first — the perception — is also crucial since it determines the kind of emotion that you have.

STUDY EXERCISES

1. Think of an example of responding to an object where the response with the mind is different from the emotional response.

2. How is an emotion defined in this section?

3. TRUE or FALSE: Emotions are always deeply felt.

4. Name the two elements to be considered with regard to
    an emotion.

. . . .

Section 2: Some Complicating Factors

The two elements to consider with regard to an emotion are the perception and the reaction. They allow us to see why it can be so hard to form our emotions aright.

For one, the perception behind an emotion may be incorrect. Then the emotion that arises from it is wrong. For example, if I perceive a glass of clear fluid as a refreshing glass of water, I will have the emotion of desire for it — even when, in reality, the glass is full of rubbing alcohol. In this case, the emotion is not reality based. It will not help me respond rightly to the object because it is based on a perception that does not see the object accurately.

We can avoid incorrect perceptions by thinking carefully about how we perceive things, but this will not avoid the problem completely. Many factors besides our thoughts contribute to our perceptions. They include habitual associations, past experiences, and attachments. Thus, even when we know with our thoughts that a perception is false, it can linger in us due to other factors that are propping it up. For example, if I find myself afraid of the dark, it is because I perceive that there is something dangerous in the dark, and even though I know with my mind that this perception is wrong, still the perception lingers, and in turn, I still have fear.

Another complicating factor is that a person can have different perceptions toward the same object. In the examples of Santa Claus and the clown, different people had different perceptions of the same object that led to divergent emotions. But it is also possible for the *same* person to have different perceptions toward the same object and thus divergent emotions in response to it. Chapter 2 gives the example of a lactose-intolerant person who has two perceptions toward ice cream. One perception sees ice cream as agreeable to the taste buds; the other perception sees it as disagreeable to the digestive system. As a result, this person has different emotions toward ice cream.

Chapter 8 gives the example of the firefighter who must endure bodily harm to save a person from a burning building. He has two perceptions toward the prospect of entering the burning building to save the person. One perception is to see it as a danger, and the other is to see it as a noble deed. Thus, the firefighter has different emotions toward entering the burning building. When one has different perceptions toward the same object and thus divergent emotions, those emotions might conflict with each other. This can be difficult and confusing and is thus another complicating factor.

Both of the conflicting perceptions or simply one of them can be wrong. Then again, both can be correct. Notice that both perceptions are correct in the examples of the lactose-intolerant person and of the firefighter. When both perceptions are correct, it shows not only that there are different sides to the same object to be considered but also that there are different layers or levels within us. The same object can be looked at differently with respect to those layers.

Thus, with respect to taste, the lactose-intolerant person perceives ice cream as pleasant, but with respect to digestion, he perceives it as unpleasant. And with respect to bodily well-being, the firefighter perceives entering a burning building as harmful, while with respect to moral integrity, he perceives it as good and noble. Even though both perceptions are correct, they lead to conflicting emotions, and so, one must use one's mind to decide which perception and emotion are to be followed in that situation. This is not always easy to do.

Another complication in getting our emotions right is that

an emotion can be too strong or too weak. The emotion might be the right emotion to have in a situation but be excessive or deficient in its strength. For example, Bill has the emotion of desire toward the success of his favorite sports team. It is OK for him to desire that his team win, but his desire is too strong. It is out of proportion with the actual importance of a sports game. Or suppose I did something wrong and I rightly have the emotion of sorrow about it, but my sorrow is too weak. I could use a greater dose of remorse.

The disproportionate strength of an emotion can be due to its underlying perception. The emotion may be too weak because one does not perceive the object with the gravity it deserves, or it may be too strong because one perceives the object as having more importance than it actually does. But there can be factors at work other than how one perceives the object. Whatever the factors, an emotion can be disproportionate in its forcefulness.

STUDY EXERCISES

1. Name three complicating factors mentioned above.

2. Come up with an example for each of these three complicating factors.

3. TRUE or FALSE: Whenever a person has two different perceptions toward an object, at least one of them must be wrong.

Section 3: The Goal of Integration

The general goal in forming our emotions is to have them work with the mind. Indeed, we want them to work so closely with the mind that we can speak of the mind and the emotions being integrated.

This integration often occurs so that both mind and emotions respond in unison to some object. For example, a mother responds to her newborn child with love that is both of the mind and of the emotions. The love she has is felt, and thus it is a felt reaction — that is, an emotion. But the love is also with the understanding of her mind. The two basic levels within her are integrated as a unified response — the response of love toward the child.

The mind and the emotions do not always work in unison. We already saw the examples of the homeless man and the sick person. Another example is when we love someone but do not like that person. We are loving the person with our minds, knowing the person to have inherent value as a human being. But what we *feel* toward the person is different. Our felt response — that is, the emotion — is not quite loving!

When the mind and the emotions are divided, we want to work for their integration as much as we can. I say "as much as we can" because, in some cases, a profound integration is not possible in this life. One reason is that we have sinful tendencies within us, especially in our emotions. We work to reduce these sinful tendencies, and we can make considerable progress in this, but they will not be completely eradicated in this life. As a result, there will always be some disordered emotions within us that do not cooperate with what our minds know is right. We should not beat ourselves up about this but should be patient and rely on God's grace.

So, with patience and with the help of God's grace, we work for integration as much as possible. To achieve this, the mind must take the lead. It has the use of reason, by which to discern what is morally good (right) versus what is morally bad (wrong). Yes, the mind can get things wrong, but still it is what governs our decision-making in the last analysis. So, its task is to reason carefully — listening, consulting, comparing, intuiting, deducting, and all the various things that reasoning does — in order to recognize correctly what is right and what is wrong. Then, in turn, we want the emotions to work with the mind, supporting it in the attainment of what is right and the avoidance of what is wrong. To the extent that we get the two working together, we are less divided and more wholehearted in what we do. Our right actions are supported, then, not only by our minds but also by our emotions. That makes us more able — and thus more free — to act rightly.

For example, consider the case when you love but do not like a person. Suppose it is someone with whom you are having a heated argument. Your mind says to love the person by not saying harsh words, but the emotion of anger within you is urging you to say something harsh to put the person in his place. If you were to have the emotion of desire for that person's well-being, it would help you to do what is right by refraining from saying the harsh words. You might still have to struggle against the urges of anger, but it would be easier to do the right thing than if you did not have the emotion of desire to help.

STUDY EXERCISES

1. TRUE or FALSE: The goal with regard to forming our emotions is to have them work in close unison with the mind.

2. TRUE or FALSE: In this life, we will never experience times when the mind and the emotions are well integrated.

3. TRUE or FALSE: In this life, we will never completely avoid times when the mind and the emotions are divided.

4. TRUE or FALSE: The more the emotions work with the mind in urging what is right, the greater our facility for performing right actions.

Section 4: The Eleven Emotions Divided into Two Groups

This book uses the list of eleven emotions found in the thought of St. Thomas Aquinas. We may divide them into two groups: those that are for helping us to attain agreeable things and those that are for helping us to avoid disagreeable things.

By calling something "agreeable," I mean that it is perceived to agree with our well-being or at least with some aspect of it. The object is desirable in some respect, for we sense that the attainment of it would be satisfying in some way. And by calling something "disagreeable," I mean that it is perceived as disagreeing with our well-being or at least some aspect of it. It is undesirable in some respect. We sense that it would cause grief or frustration in some way.

Notice that the context is our striving for the fullness of life — that is, for complete well-being. The mind is naturally ordered toward identifying what is true and good so we might attain our fulfillment in the true and the good. Ultimately, we find this fulfillment in God, since He is the source of all that is true and good and is truth and goodness itself. The emotions are also part of this pursuit. Based on our perceptions, the emotions work to help us attain things that are agreeable to our fulfillment and to avoid things that are disagreeable to our fulfillment.

The emotions that are for attaining agreeable things are liking (or love), desire, joy, hope, and daring. The last two — hope and daring — arise only when attaining an agreeable thing is perceived to entail some complicating factor. With hope and daring, the complicating factor will be some kind of obstacle or difficulty that must be overcome to attain the agreeable thing. The first three — liking, desire, and joy — occur whether or not there is a complicating factor. The emotions that are for avoiding disagreeable things are disliking (or hate), aversion, sorrow, fear, despair, and anger. The last three — fear, despair, and anger — arise only when avoiding a disagreeable thing is perceived to entail some complicating factor. With fear, despair, and anger, the complicating factor varies. The first three — disliking, aversion, and sorrow — occur regardless of whether there is a complicating factor in the effort to avoid a disagreeable thing.

Some of the words for emotions also refer to acts of the will (where the will is the mind's free response to things). For instance, the word *hope* can refer to an emotion or to an act of the will (or even to a virtue, for that matter). Sometimes we have the emotion of hope, but not hope as an act of the will. This happens, for example, when we tell ourselves not to get our hopes up. The emotion is arising, but the mind is refusing to hope. And sometimes we hope with the will when there is no emotion of hope. This is a case of hoping against hope. I mention this to avoid misunderstanding. When I mention hope or another name for an emotion that can also refer to an act of the will, I am referring only to the emotion. So, if I mention despair, I am referring only to the emotion — that is, to the felt reaction — and I am not saying whether or not there is an act of despair by the will.

Because pursuing agreeable things and avoiding disagreeable ones are two sides of the same coin, we can often convert one into the other. For instance, if I perceive a burning building as disagreeable to my well-being, I can also perceive the avoidance of it as agreeable. Still, the pursuit of agreeable things is more fundamental than the avoidance of disagreeable things. Thus, avoiding disagreeable things is for the sake of attaining agreeable ones and not vice versa.

. . . .

STUDY EXERCISES

1. Give an example of something you find agreeable, whether superficial or profound.

2. Give an example of something you find disagreeable. Again, it can be superficial or profound.

3. Name the emotions that are felt reactions to things perceived as agreeable.

4. Name the emotions that are felt reactions to things perceived as disagreeable.

5. Which emotions arise only when there is a complicating factor in attaining agreeable things, and which arise only when there is a complicating factor in avoiding disagreeable things?

6. TRUE or FALSE: The avoidance of disagreeable things is an end in itself.

. . . .

Section 5: Liking, Desire, and Joy

When I define the emotions here and in the following sections, I will describe the reaction that is felt toward an object and how that object is perceived in order to elicit this reaction. That is, the definition will have the two elements of an emotion: the reaction and the perception. I will then offer examples, the first being relatively superficial and the second more profound.

> **Liking (or love)**: The agreement (resonance, harmony) felt toward an object that is perceived as agreeable to (in alignment with, conducive to) some aspect of one's well-being.

> **Desire**: The attraction felt toward an object that is perceived as agreeable and as not yet attained.

> **Joy**: The elation (delight, satisfaction) felt in response to an object that is perceived as agreeable and as attained.

Since pursuing what is agreeable is the fundamental aim, the emotion of liking is the most fundamental emotion, and all the other emotions follow from it. How valuable it is, then, for us to perceive correctly what is agreeable to us and thus to like the right things!

The other two emotions of desire and joy follow immediately from the emotion of liking. If the thing we like is not yet attained, we have the emotion of desire toward it. And if the thing we like is attained, we have the emotion of joy over it.

It is important to note that, while we define the emotions in terms of what is agreeable or disagreeable to *ourselves*, we can also have emotions with regard to *another's well-being*. We are able to identify with the people we care about, and so we find something agreeable to ourselves if it is agreeable to them and we find something disagreeable to ourselves if it is disagreeable to them. Thus, a father will have the emotion of liking for his son's maturation into a good young man. The son's maturation is agreeable to the son and, in turn, is agreeable to the father, who cares about him.

Here is a relatively superficial example of these emotions. Greg *likes* strawberry ice cream, and not having it, he experiences the emotion of *desire* for it. He goes to the store, buys some, and eats it. Now he has the emotion of *joy*.

Next, consider a more profound example of these emotions. Greta *likes* to spend time with God in prayer. After a busy day that has filled her mind with many worries, she has a *desire* for prayer. So, she goes to the local church and sits before the Blessed Sacrament. In a few moments, she experiences a deep *joy*.

. . . .

STUDY EXERCISES

1. Think of an example in which the emotions of liking, desire, and joy play out. (When an example is asked for here and in the following sections, do not worry whether it is superficial or profound. Either will do.)

2. Think of another example in which one experiences these emotions with respect to what is agreeable to another person's well-being.

. . . .

Section 6: Disliking, Aversion, and Sorrow

> **Disliking (or hatred)**: The disagreement (dissonance) felt in response to an object that is perceived as disagreeable to (contrary to, incompatible with) some aspect of one's well-being.

> **Aversion**: The repulsion felt toward an object that is perceived as disagreeable and as possibly coming upon oneself.

> **Sorrow**: The deepening of disliking felt toward an object that is perceived as being disagreeable and as having come upon oneself; that is, one perceives the object as a problem, where the word *problem* refers to the situation wherein a disagreeable thing has come upon oneself.

Just as there is often a progression from liking something to desiring it and then to enjoying it once it is attained, so there is often a progression from disliking something to having aversion toward it and then being sorrowful because it has occurred. But unlike the first progression, the progression from disliking to sorrow is not favorable, and the emotions involved work to prevent it.

Thus, when I dislike something, I want to avoid it. If the disagreeable thing is at a distance, I need not pay much attention to it. If it draws near and there is a chance it will come upon me, however, I experience the emotion of aversion, which moves me to avoid it. Then, if I do not avoid it and it instead falls upon me, I have sorrow.

Sorrow amplifies — that is, it turns up the volume on — our disliking of the disagreeable thing. Our disliking screams out its displeasure, so to speak. This is what is meant by saying that sorrow deepens our disliking of the thing. As I will explain more in the next section, this deepened disliking prevents complacency about the problem, and it leads us to do something about the problem.

Consider a relatively superficial example of these emotions. Alex plays baseball and *dislikes* losing. He is playing in a game, and as his team heads into the final innings, they are down a few runs. It looks as if the team will lose. This prospect of losing gives rise to *aversion* in Alex, and so he tries even harder to avoid a loss. But his team still loses, and so he has *sorrow*.

Here is a more profound example of these emotions. Anna *dislikes* it when homeless people suffer from the cold. As winter approaches, she knows that this is likely to happen, so she experiences an *aversion* toward it. This leads her to volunteer with a local charity that helps the homeless. Sometimes when she is volunteering, she comes across a homeless person shivering on the streets, and she is *sorrowful*.

. . . .

STUDY EXERCISES

1. Think of an example in which the emotions of disliking, aversion, and sorrow play out.

2. Think of another example in which one experiences these emotions with respect to what is disagreeable to another person's well-being.

. . . .

Section 7: More on Sorrow

We need to say more about the emotion of sorrow, since it is hard to understand. Here we will hit on some of the main points, which are covered in more detail in chapter 5. For one, the generic term *sorrow* is less than ideal to cover a wide variety of experiences. That is, there are different versions of this emotion, such as discomfort, suffering, pain, grief, sadness, mourning, and disappointment. All count here as the emotion of sorrow. Each arises from some disagreeable thing coming upon oneself (or upon someone whom one cares about).

The approach to the emotions in this book sees every emotion as having a good purpose. Each can help us to attain what is truly agreeable or to avoid what is truly disagreeable. Sorrow is no exception. It arises when we perceive that something disagreeable has happened. The reaction of sorrow is to deepen our disliking of the disagreeable thing that has happened. This does two helpful things: It makes us aware, or more aware, of the problem, and it motivates us to do something about it. (Remember from the definition of *sorrow* that the term *problem* is shorthand for the situation in which something disagreeable has happened.)

An illustrative example is when the experience of pain leads a person to go to the doctor. The pain (a version of sorrow) makes the person aware of a problem, and it motivates the person to deal with it. Moreover, to know how to deal with the health problem, the doctor diagnoses its cause.

Consider a relatively superficial example of this emotion. Willy experiences *soreness* in his knee. This *makes him aware* of the fact that he strained his knee from the vigorous bike ride he took yesterday. The soreness *motivates* him to take measures to let his knee heal by temporarily avoiding bike rides and any other strenuous exercise involving his knee.

Next, consider a more profound example. Wanda is *saddened* to see that something she said hurt her friend Joan. This *makes her aware* that her words were out of place. In turn, she is *motivated* to apologize to Joan and to be more careful with her words in the future.

For sorrow to serve a good purpose, it must be reality based. One can have sorrow over a problem that is not real but only perceived, and in this case, the sorrow is not helpful. For example, a man mistakenly diagnosed with a rare blood disease will have sorrow over that. But since the diagnosis was wrong, his sorrow is not helpful toward avoiding the disease, given that the disease is not there! Also, to be helpful (or most helpful), the sorrow should avoid being too strong or too weak. We can be too sad about something, such as by mourning a mistake too strongly, and we can fail to be sad enough, such as by not having sufficient sorrow for a sin.

To appreciate the usefulness of sorrow, it helps to see that sorrow is not itself the problem. The problem is what one is sorrowful about. Thus, when one has pain (such as from burning one's hand), that is different from the painful thing (the flame that burned the hand). And when one suffers (say, from the loss of a loved one), the suffering is different from what caused it (the loss of a loved one). Sometimes we conflate the emotion of sorrow with the problem (i.e., the disagreeable thing that has happened), and so we speak of sorrow as the problem that needs to be avoided. To be sure, sometimes sorrow is to be avoided. Yet, to speak more precisely, the problem is not the sorrow but what is causing the sorrow — namely, the problem. Sorrow is good because it makes us responsive to a problem in order to do what can be done to resolve it.

We need not, nor should we, always embrace sorrow and never try to avoid it. The primary way of trying to get rid of sorrow is to resolve its underlying cause. But even when the problem causing the sorrow cannot be completely resolved in this life (all problems are resolved in heaven), one need not continue suffering from the problem. Thus, a person with pain from an illness that cannot be cured can rightly use medications to eliminate the pain. And even if the illness can be cured over time, one can seek to eliminate the pain. Recall that sorrow works to make us aware of and motivated against a problem. So, if one is aware of a problem and is motivated to address it, sorrow is no longer necessary. Or if there is nothing that can be done about the problem, the sorrow no longer has a purpose.

Still, there are times when it is constructive to sit with our sorrow so as to deepen our disliking of a problem. This can help us to maintain a healthy awareness of the problem and a sufficient animus against it. And as chapter 5 explains, sorrow can be healing and redemptive by deepening our dislike of the fallen condition of our world and by deepening our repudiation of sin as its root cause.

A final observation to make is that, while sorrow itself is not the problem, it can lead to a problem. Again, sorrow motivates us to deal with a problem, but what if we deal with the problem in the wrong way? Then that wrong way of dealing with the problem becomes a new problem! For example, José is hurt from being betrayed by a friend. The hurt motivates him to avoid this problem in the future, but he decides to avoid this problem in the future by never having a close friend again. His way of resolving the original problem leads to a new problem.

....

STUDY EXERCISES
1. Think of an example in which sorrow makes a person aware of a problem and motivates the person to address the problem.

2. Give an example in which a person's sorrow is not reality based.

3. Give an example in which a person's sorrow is either too strong or too weak.

4. Give an example of someone being moved by sorrow to deal with a problem but in the wrong way.

Section 8: The Emotion of Fear

Fear: The heightened awareness felt toward an object that it is perceived as disagreeable and as difficult to avoid — in other words, the perception is of a danger.

Fear is similar to aversion in that both entail perceiving the possibility that a disagreeable thing may come upon oneself. But there is a complicating factor in the perception behind fear. Aversion simply perceives that a disagreeable thing may happen, but fear additionally perceives the complication that avoiding that thing will be difficult. In this sense, the disagreeable thing threatens to happen, or, in other words, there is a danger that it will happen.

With aversion, the added element is not needed. For example, I dislike peppermint ice cream, so if someone offers me some by putting a bowl of it in front of me, I have aversion toward it. But I do not have fear, since avoiding the peppermint ice cream is not difficult to do.

What good purpose does fear serve? Its reaction is to heighten our awareness of the danger at hand. Thus, our senses and thinking are put on alert toward the danger, so that we are more focused on finding a way to avoid it. In short, fear is helpful by making us alert to a danger so that we may better avoid it.

Consider this relatively superficial example. Zoe is hosting some friends and making them dinner. She has chosen to make a dish that, while very tasty, is difficult to make. There is a danger that it might not come out well. *Fearing* that possibility, she focuses very carefully on preparing it.

Here is a more profound example. Zach needs to have a difficult conversation with a friend. He knows that there is a danger that the conversation will not go well, and *fearing* that, he prepares carefully for the conversation, so that it may be constructive.

Notice that fear can be wrong by not being reality based. For example, a person can be afraid of a clown even though the clown is not a danger. Also, fear can go wrong by being too excessive or deficient. For instance, one should have fear when driving on snowy roads, so as to be alert to the danger of a crash. If one is deficient in fear, the person may be insufficiently alert. On the other hand, when fear is excessive, it can result in panic or paralysis. Of course, neither is very helpful.

STUDY EXERCISES

1. Give an example of fear being helpful.

2. Give an example of fear not being helpful because it is not reality based.

3. Give an example of fear not being helpful because it is either excessive or deficient.

4. TRUE or FALSE: Fear is always bad to have.

Section 9: The Emotion of Anger

Anger: The protest felt toward an object that is perceived as disagreeable and as having unjustly occurred — in other words, the perception is that an injustice has occurred.

Anger is similar to sorrow in that both entail a perception that something disagreeable has happened. But there is a complicating factor in the perception behind anger. Whereas sorrow simply perceives that a disagreeable thing happened, anger additionally perceives the complication that it was unjust for that thing to have happened. It should not have happened. Someone or something is to blame for its having taken place.

Sorrow can occur without attaching such blame to the problem that has arisen. For example, if a bee stings me, I will have pain (which is, again, a version of sorrow). But if I do not blame the bee or myself (say, for going near the beehive) or someone or something else (say, the person on whose property is the beehive), then I do not have anger. But if I blame the bee, myself, or the property owner, then I have anger. The anger protests what happened rather than simply accepting it as unfortunate. What happened is not only a problem but an injustice.

The reaction of anger is to register a protest against what has happened. Anger is helpful when this protest keeps us from accepting an injustice as OK and leads us, to the extent possible, to work toward righting the wrong done.

Consider this relatively superficial example. Joanne is *angry* that she forgot to call her good friend on her friend's birthday, which was yesterday. Considering this unacceptable, she does not simply move on but tries to make amends by calling her friend today.

Here is a more profound example. Joe is *angry* that his younger brother was ridiculed at college for his Catholic faith. Joe's objection to this leads him to talk with his brother about how to deal with and respond to the ridicule.

As with the other emotions, anger can serve a good purpose only if it is reality based and only insofar as it is neither too strong nor too weak. Anger easily goes astray in both ways. Often it is not reality based, such as when someone gets angry over a perceived slight that was not actually intended as a slight at all. And even when anger is justified in the sense that it is reality based (i.e., the perceived injustice is real), it can still be too strong or too weak. For example, Barbara has a teenage daughter who did what she knew was wrong. If Barbara's anger over this is too strong, she might give her daughter a punishment that is too extreme. But if Barbara's anger is too weak, she may not have the zeal to correct her daughter as she should.

While anger is based on perceiving that an injustice has occurred, sometimes we get angry when an injustice has not yet occurred. For example, Bob is angry because someone threatened harm against his wife, even though the harm has not happened thus far. In a way, even the fact that the harm is being threatened is a disagreeable thing that has already happened. Bob sees that his wife should not have to deal with this situation; hence, he has anger over it.

STUDY EXERCISES

1. Give an example of someone having an anger that is reality based.

2. Give an example of someone having an anger that is not reality based.

3. Give an example of someone having a reality-based anger that is either too strong or too weak.

Section 10: Hope, Despair, and Daring

The remaining three emotions (hope, daring, and despair) apply when we want something (that is, we find something agreeable and have desire for it), but an obstacle — great or small, simple or complex — stands between us and what we want. To attain the desired thing, the obstacle must be overcome. This is the complicating factor at work with these three emotions. When we perceive that the obstacle can be overcome, we have the emotion of hope. When we perceive that it cannot be overcome, we have the emotion of despair. I will explain how the emotion of daring comes into play after giving the definitions of these three emotions. Also, though I give the definition of despair here, I will treat it in the next section.

> **Hope:** The uplifting of spirits one feels toward an object that is perceived as agreeable, difficult to attain, and yet attainable — that is, the perception is that a difficulty or obstacle between oneself and the desired object can be overcome.

> **Despair:** The deflation of one's spirits felt in response to an object that is perceived as agreeable and yet impossible to attain — that is, the perception that an obstacle in the way of the desired object is insurmountable.

> **Daring:** The emboldening of one's spirits felt toward an object that is perceived as a surmountable obstacle to what one hopes to attain.

The emotion of daring was not discussed in the chapters of this book, although it is related to the resolve spoken of in chapter 2 and the overcoming of sloth in chapter 6. Daring presupposes the emotion of hope. Whereas hope is felt toward a goal when we think that the obstacle in the way is surmountable, daring is felt toward the obstacle itself. We can especially appreciate this emotion when we have a role in overcoming the obstacle in our way.

For example, five-year-old Johnny cannot reach the jar of cookies on the shelf, since it is too high. He is ready to despair of getting a cookie, but then his older sister, who is nearby, says, "Hold on, Johnny. I'll get you a cookie." The obstacle is now surmountable by means of his sister. Johnny has no role in overcoming the obstacle, but he still has hope. In contrast, suppose that Johnny's sister is not around, but he does not despair of getting the cookie. He thinks he can overcome the obstacle. Thinking this, he has hope, and this leads to daring. With the emotion of daring, he does not shrink from the challenge but, instead, grabs a nearby chair, places it below the shelf, and climbs up on it to reach the cookie jar. The usefulness of daring is easier to see in the latter case, when one must play a role in overcoming the obstacle. It then gives a person boldness in confronting the obstacle.

For hope and daring to be useful, the usual caveats apply. Thus, hope is not helpful if it is not reality based. This happens when hope is based on incorrectly perceiving an obstacle as surmountable when, in reality, the obstacle is not. And even if one's hope is reality based, so must be one's daring. One can wrongly think that one can conquer an obstacle even when one cannot. Also, one can be too daring, having an excessive boldness toward overcoming an obstacle. Thus, one might try to overcome an obstacle by oneself when others' help is needed to do so. Or one can be not daring enough. Thus, one is not bold enough in doing one's part to overcome an obstacle.

Consider this relatively superficial example of hope and daring. Mazie *hopes* to beat her brother at a game of ping pong, even though he is very good. So, with *daring* she challenges him to a game and plays hard against him.

Here is a more profound example. Marco wants to be a paramedic, but he knows it will be challenging. He must undertake training, and the nature of the work is itself difficult. Still, he *hopes* to become a paramedic, and he *dares* to do what is needed to be a good one.

. . . .

STUDY EXERCISES

1. Give an example of hoping for something when one's agency is not needed to overcome the obstacle.

2. Give an example of hoping for something when one's agency is needed to overcome the obstacle.

3. TRUE or FALSE: Every case of hope is helpful.

. . . .

Section 11: More on the Emotion of Despair

As noted in the preceding section, the emotion of despair arises when one sees as insurmountable an obstacle in the way of what one desires. One perceives that the obstacle cannot be overcome either by one's own efforts or with the available support of others.

If we liken hope to the wind that fills one's sails when working toward a goal, despair is what takes the wind out of one's sails. Can such an emotion ever be good? Yes. Sometimes the obstacle in the way of a goal is truly insurmountable, and thus, one should stop trying to attain the goal. Then hope is not useful, for it would keep driving one toward the unattainable goal. On the other hand, despair is useful, for it takes away the motivation to work toward the goal. One can then more easily let go of that goal and move on.

For example, Joe has the dream of being a fighter pilot, but then his eyesight deteriorates, so he is no longer able to become one. His poor vision becomes an insurmountable obstacle to his dream. As painful as it may be, he needs to move on. In such a situation, he needs to stop trying. Despair is useful then. It usefully takes the wind out of his sails, so that he pauses and is given the opportunity to see that he needs to let go of the goal and move on.

As noted in chapter 6, when one must despair of something essential for human fulfillment, one should still hope to attain it in heaven. For example, bodily health is essential for fulfillment, but if Alicia learns that her cancer is terminal, she should despair of recovering her health. She has made reasonable attempts to be cured, but the time has come to stop seeking a cure. That will, of course, be difficult and heartbreaking. Yet the emotion of despair helps Alicia to let go and to stop seeking a cure. Even while she goes through the difficult process of letting go of her health in this life, however, she should not despair of it in the life to come. She should hope to have it for eternity in heaven.

Again, when we stop hoping for a goal that cannot be attained, we can move on to other things that can be beneficially done. Thus, in the difficult case of Alicia and her terminal cancer, her despair of a cure allows her to move on to other things, such as preparing for death by receiving the sacraments, saying goodbye to loved ones, and making whatever amends are needed.

Of course, the usual caveats apply. The despair must be reality based. If one perceives the obstacle to be insurmountable, whereas it is surmountable, then the despair is not reality based, and it is not helpful. In this case, one should not give up but should have hope and push on with daring.

As for despair being too strong or too weak, this can happen when one sees the loss of a goal as being more significant or less significant than it really is. For example, Christie is trying out for her high school basketball team, but she places too much significance on whether she will make the team. So, after she is cut from the team during tryouts, her despair is too strong. Her spirits are too deflated. On the other hand, suppose Wally's girlfriend, Grace, breaks up with him and even tells him that she regrets ever knowing him. If Wally then thinks, "OK, Grace will not be my girlfriend, but we can still be friends," then he is not deflated enough by despair. The significance of the rupture in their relationship is greater than he realizes. He needs to give up on having Grace not only as a girlfriend but also as a friend.

Consider this relatively superficial example of despair. After going to an impressive piano concert, Peter dreams of being a professional pianist. But eventually, he *despairs* of this goal, for he comes to see that he lacks a facility for the piano and that he does not have sufficient time to practice.

Here is a more profound example. Patricia is a small-business owner, and in the past couple of years, her business has been struggling. After crunching the numbers and seeing that her business can no longer meet its costs, she *despairs* of keeping her business open and decides to close it down.

. . . .

STUDY EXERCISES

1. TRUE or FALSE: It is always bad to have the emotion of despair.

2. Come up with an example of despair being helpful.

3. Come up with an example of despair being unhelpful.

. . . .

About the Author

Abbot Austin G. Murphy has been a Benedictine monk of St. Procopius Abbey in Lisle, Illinois, since 1996. He was ordained to the priesthood in 2004, and from 2010 to 2024, he was the abbot of St. Procopius Abbey. Besides the theological training, especially in monastic theology, that he received during his initial formation as a monk, he studied at the Dominican House of Studies for the priesthood and for an MA in theology. He earned a PhD in theology at the University of Notre Dame in 2016, focusing on the thought of Saint Augustine.